THE WORD ON THE STREET

The Word on the Street

PERFORMING THE SCRIPTURES
IN THE URBAN CONTEXT

Stanley P. Saunders
Charles L. Campbell

WILLIAM B. EERDMANS PUBLISHING COMPANY
GRAND RAPIDS, MICHIGAN / CAMBRIDGE, U.K.

© 2000 Wm. B. Eerdmans Publishing Co.
255 Jefferson Ave. S.E., Grand Rapids, Michigan 49503 /
P.O. Box 163, Cambridge CB3 9PU U.K.
All rights reserved

Printed in the United States of America

05 04 03 02 01 00   7 6 5 4 3 2 1

Library of Congress Cataloging-in-Publication Data

Saunders, Stanley P.
The word on the street: performing the scriptures in the urban context /
Stanley P. Saunders, Charles L. Campbell.
p.   cm.
Includes bibliographical references.
ISBN 0-8028-4393-X (pbk.: alk. paper)
1. Church work with the homeless — Georgia — Atlanta.
2. Open Door Community.   I. Campbell, Charles L.   II. Title.
BV4456.S38   2000
261.8'325'09758231 — dc21

00-023127

For

The Open Door Community

*whose daily performance of Scripture
brings life in the midst of death*

Contents

CONTENTS

Contents

Foreword

Antonio Gramsci, that daring and much-imprisoned Italian sociologist, devised the phrase "organic intellectual." He intends the phrase to refer to working academics who are intentionally connected to movements of social transformation and revolution, who permit their actual engagement in such movements to influence, shape, and provide categories for their academic research. Gramsci, moreover, intends the phrase as a contrast to and judgment upon intellectuals who carry on their work in a social vacuum, as though the categories, purposes, and judgments concerning their research were intrinsic to the process itself without any larger reference. Whereas the latter are fundamentally irrelevant to the real world, "organic intellectuals" matter decisively to social reality, because transforming and revolutionary developments in society depend upon hard, critical thinking as the biting edge to social engagement.

I find Gramsci's phrasing helpful in appreciating this present volume, precisely because Charles Campbell and Stanley Saunders are indeed "organic intellectuals" whose critical work in their respective academic disciplines is related to, informed by, and in the service of the social transformation to which they are committed. I suppose it is correct to say that all of us engaged in theological research who take the church seriously are more or less organically connected, but these two young colleagues are visibly, practically, and intentionally connected to the movement in ways that suggest a different model of work and self-understanding.

The title of this book is more cunning than it appears at first glance, because it intends to speak of a very particular word on a very particular street. The particular word is the gospel word of the Bible, with its insistence that the God of the Bible, in Jesus of Nazareth, has changed everything and made all things new. The street, in turn, is a very particular street. It happens that the "Open Door," the venue for this "organic engagement," is on a street named Ponce de Leon, or as we say, "The Ponce." The particularity of the street is found, however, not in that ancient and romantic name, but in the particular lives that are lived there, lives that are compounded of deep need and deep hurt and indeed deep hope that refuses to give in. That street "where cross the crowded ways of life" is a street of the hungry homeless who are bodily present to the busy commerce, traffic, trade, investment, and enforcement that colludes in the production of need and hurt, but that pays no attention to the carriers of that need and hurt.

The question that is endlessly posed by this interface of *word* and *street* is whether connection can be made between the two. On the face of it, there is no place hungrier for this word than this street (though one might argue that the hunger for the word is equally poignant on other, better-looking streets that are peopled by malls, banks, and "working churches"). It is a wonderment whether the word will provide any news that could be "good" on this street where the powers of death, despair, and abandonment are so palpable. It is the insistence of this present "word-book" by these organic intellectuals that the word is indeed good news here, because it asserts that the palpable death and despair is not the final reality. But this book is not singularly a "word-book." It is, I think even more, a "street-book"; it makes the relentless claim that it takes this street of broken bodies and nearly crushed spirits to give access to the word that makes all things new. Quite clearly it is the exposure to and engagement with this street that permits Saunders and Campbell to attend to the word in the decisive way that they do.

The interface of *word* and *street* is nicely put together in their aphorism "Street Readings/Reading the Streets." That way of putting the interface reminds me of the parallel statement, most often attributed to Karl Barth, that we should proceed with the Bible in one hand and the newspaper in the other. The point of that statement, of course, is to insist that the Bible must be related to what is going on in the world. The transposition from "Bible/newspaper" to "Bible/street," however, is a huge and telling maneuver. For these authors would surely insist, and rightly, that reading the newspaper is no adequate substitute for reading the street, for the newspaper is already a purified, purged reading of the street that is cleaned up to serve the interests and sensibilities of those of us who know little of the street and who want, even less, to know about the street. The slogan "Bible and newspaper" may in fact represent the ideological self-deception of much of the theological enterprise and the awareness of the church as we have lived in it — an awareness that is something of a protected cocoon away from the human reality of the street. Indeed it does not matter much if one reads the local *Journal-Constitution* or *The New York Times* as a paper of record; establishment interests have already cleansed everything, renamed everything, and invented euphemisms to distance and protect us from the truth of the street. Against such an idealistic misrepresentation, the street, as this book shows, plunges people of the word into the harsh, resilient, bodily traffic of humanness, a bodily reality that is an inconvenience, but that is shown here to be commensurate with the bodily reality of incarnational faith.

The bid of this book, in the wake of William Stringfellow, is to make a beginning on a new mode of "public theology." As the reader will know, the whole matter of "public theology" in current discussion is a hugely disputatious subject, given a secularism and pluralism that have "emptied" the "public square" of theological substance. As a consequence, most of what passes for public theology turns out to be exceedingly conservative, in the defense of the status quo, suggesting that anyone who departs from the old rational, capitalist consensus is a little flaky and is not to be taken seriously by those in the know who must act responsibly. Such a prism for public theology is, predictably, deeply establishment in its orientation.

The counter to such a sorry notion of public theology has been especially voiced by Stanley Hauerwas in his work, which is too readily caricatured and dismissed as "sectarian." Hauerwas's contribution, as I understand it, is to insist that the church, led by the word, must go full throttle in its own discernment and convictions, without accommodation to establishment interests. Whatever may finally be made of Hauerwas's own work, it is clear that his passion and freedom are important ingredients for this present work. It is clear, moreover, that Saunders and Campbell have no interest in either accommodationist public theology or in a sectarian alternative that retreats before public scrutiny.

Rather, this public theology works in the categories given by the word, and proceeds to show that these categories of discernment, interpretation, and action are perfectly credible in making sense of public reality and in authorizing actions and policies that make sense and make human in a troubled urban society. This way of doing public theology is without apology, defensiveness, or embarrassment. It is also without much accommodation to conventional wisdom and conventional perception, because it dares to suggest that such conventions are likely to be distorting seductions. These authors understand well that these fresh categories for public theology are not easy or obvious, and are sure to be resisted and contested. But to be contested is exactly what advocates like Campbell and Saunders most want, to be contested so that gospel claims for the street are in dispute alongside market claims for the street that must also be brought into dispute.

That of course is why these authors are open to "street preaching." The enterprise of street preaching is neither wacko nuttiness nor exhibitionism; it is the joining of a contest in which the unexamined conventions of dominant society do not go uncontested and prevail by default.

I understand the importance of street preaching to be the urgency of contested reality. There will be many readers of this volume — many preachers among them — who have no intention of ever preaching on the street. If, however, street preaching means to engage in contested claims in the midst of the material, bodily reality of the street, then I wonder if preaching inside the church, here inside the church building, might more fully meet the demands of street preaching if the preacher (and the congregation) understood that street preaching, as distinct from conventional church preaching, entails a *willingness to contest and be contested* amidst *bodily reality.* My impression is that church preaching tends to be safe and consequently innocuous, not because it is in a church building, but because it tends not to be disputatious enough and not to be informed by the bodily reality of brokenness so evident on the street. Were church preaching to take on such qualities of street preaching, the church might more readily do public theology. I have no doubt that serious public theology finally must be done by preachers, not by scholars removed from the concrete daily life of the church. This public theology, moreover, has as a critical task the debunking of the plausibility structures of much of our society. It occurs to me that the relationship between conventional church preaching and street preaching is not unlike the "church theology" and "prophetic theology" distinguished in the *Kairos Document* of some years ago in the Reformed tradition of South Africa. That is, street preaching may more readily do what is the proper task of church preaching, just as "prophetic theology" is the proper work of "church theology." In both cases, what is required is the move from an idealistic enterprise that engages in denial, to the bodily world where the gifts and demands of the gospel are so powerfully operative.

The burden of this sort of public theology, however, is not primarily critical and disputatious, though such requirements are always present. This public theology, at its best, is rather declarative and affirmative in a kind of courageous chutzpah that asserts its own claims freely and without compromise. I am struck, repeatedly, by the ways in which this book appeals to gesture, hint, sign, and sacrament. The church, in its contestation, must always work in such a way, because the dominant and defining categories of reality, mistaken as they are, occupy a lot of space and administer a lot of hardware. In the face of such formidable force, the claims of this public theology are not easy or obvious or readily persuasive. These claims must always be made from the underside, in a way that seeks to enter the unguarded pores of dominant assumptions. Thus in an exposition of the narrative of the triumphal entry in Matthew, Stan and Chuck speak easily of "street theater," of acting out in public before an unpersuaded constituency a truth about Jesus that is counter to commonly assumed reality. The theater of truth on the street has a playful, teasing quality to it, but the tease has conviction and the play has authority. It lives at the edge of fiction, for the claims of the word, if genuinely heard, always sound like fiction to the powers of this age.

"Street theater" abounds in this manuscript:

- Little Carson is baptized, a little theater of water and formula, and his father dares to term it "a death in the family," a death to all that is old and deathly and hopeless. The community watches the performance, shares in the theater, and as able, dies the death that is accomplished dramatically in and through the water.

- A dispute arose on the street about coffee, doughnuts, and ownership, who would eat, who would drink, who would control. What might have been an altercation, according to the assumptions of the market, turned out to be a genuine sharing. The community was watching and they saw, one more time, the drama of bread and wine and brokenness and healing and nourishment and all things new. One had to be watching to notice, or one might have missed the sacramental moment.

- A most outrageous claim from the word is resurrection. These authors speak of "resurrection imagination" that "happens in the places where suffering and glory, humanity and divinity, spirit and flesh, presence and absence are embraced." It will make some of us nervous to link "resurrection" to "imagination," because then it may be less than "real" and "physical." But imagination is the capacity to see differently, to see that Easter is not just an ancient Sunday enterprise, but rather it is an endless, concrete surprise on the street.

For starters, that gives baptism, Eucharist, and resurrection as a prism for public theology. The bread is thin and the wine is poured out, and Easter is fragile news wherever it is told and trusted. None of it is compelling, unless one is on the street to see it, unless one is free to discern it, unless some are bold enough to sing it and say it. This act of evangelical reconstrual is daring and always uphill, but in no other way will the street be seen to be congruent with the word.

As a colleague who has watched these younger colleagues grow in freedom and courage, I am profoundly grateful for this book. As a colleague who is not very "organic" in the terms that Campbell and Saunders embody so well, I am moved by what they have seen and shared. I am chastened by it, but also energized. This book invites a rethink and a reconstrual of many dimensions of the church. Not least, of course, is its chastening, energizing word to seminaries and to those who engage in theological education. The summons for teachers and scholars is to be organically engaged. And that cannot happen effectively until we are present to the bodily truth and free enough for contestation. These strange gestures and signs that well up on the street, that seem like fiction, remind in powerful ways that the deep "fiction" which besets us is in fact our dominant categories of "truth."

The book offers a stunning, characteristically evangelical transposition so that what has been true is seen to be fiction and what seemed like fiction turns out to be defining truth. That odd exchange makes us much like Pilate in his wonderment about truth (John 18:38). It is instructive that the question is asked by the Roman governor just a chapter away from the "piercing" that happened on the street, in the public arena where the body of Jesus contested the claims of tradition and empire (John 19:34). Campbell and Saunders hold the question of truth close to the pain on the street, and invite us all to this odd place of newness.

WALTER BRUEGGEMANN
Columbia Theological Seminary
July 15, 1999

Acknowledgments

Walter Brueggemann, a constant guide and support to his junior colleagues, not only first encouraged us to submit these essays and sermons for publication, but also volunteered to contribute the Foreword to the book.

William B. Eerdmans, Jr., saw the potential for a book in our occasional writings and enthusiastically encouraged this project; and Jennifer Hoffman, Assistant Managing Editor at Eerdmans, graciously and efficiently facilitated the editing and production of the book.

James Hudnut-Beumler, Dean of the Faculty at Columbia Seminary, has supported us both in our hours away from campus and in our experimental courses on the streets of Atlanta.

Students in our courses have come to class at 5:45 A.M., slept on sidewalks, been placed under arrest, sung hymns in subway stations, read Scripture at shelters, and preached on the streets. We have learned much from their patience, their courage, and their reflections.

Jonathan Kaplan, one of our students at Columbia, prepared the bibliography and the indices.

Ginger Kaney and Dewey Merritt, formerly of the Urban Training Organization of Atlanta, allowed Chuck to share in their work during his sabbatical and taught him much about Atlanta's public housing projects.

Our friend and mentor, Ed Loring, one of the founders of the Open Door Community, has spent countless hours introducing us to the streets of Atlanta and helping us reflect on our experiences. As those who know Ed will recognize, he is in many ways a co-author of this book.

Many homeless people in Atlanta have welcomed us into their lives and served as very patient teachers for two seminary professors out of their element.

The Open Door Community has changed our lives, nurtured our discipleship, and served as the womb out of which this project was born. Several members of the Open Door — Gladys Rustay, Elizabeth Dede, Murphy Davis, and Ed Loring — also read and commented upon portions of the manuscript. Finally, the Open Door gave us permission to reprint most of the essays in this book, which originally appeared in the community's newspaper, *Hospitality*.

Our wives, Brenda Smith and Dana Campbell, and our children, Carson Smith-Saunders and Lydia and Thomas Campbell, have not only been patient with our constant scheming and our hours away from home, but have actively encouraged our work and regularly joined us "on the street."

To all of these persons we are profoundly grateful.

Somebody Lives Here
Etching with aquatint; 16″ × 12″; © 1996 Christina Bray

Sin, Grace, and the Basement Door

At 6:20 A.M. nine of us stood in a circle at the Open Door Community and heard the words of the prophet Micah: "What does Yahweh require of you but to do justice, and to love kindness, and to walk humbly with your God?" (Micah 6:8). Then, following a prayer, we boarded the van and drove to Butler Street C.M.E. Church, where we planned to share breakfast with the homeless people waiting for us there.

On this particular morning, however, the line of men and women gathered for breakfast was disorderly. As I unlocked the basement door, the rest of our group was trying to bring some order to the line. When these efforts failed, the decision was made to return to the Open Door without serving the meal. I relocked the door, and everyone except Ed Loring and I climbed back into the van and left. Ed and I remained behind and listened to the anger and frustration of the hungry people who would receive no breakfast that morning. "I've been here waiting since 5:00!" "I'm hungry, man, and I've got to go to work!" "And you call yourselves Christians!" "It's not fair. I wasn't causing any trouble. Why can't I get something to eat?" All Ed and I could reply was, "No, it's not fair, but we have to have some order to serve the breakfast. We know we're sinners. We'll be back in the morning."

Although this was my first time to go to the Butler Street Breakfast on one of those rare occasions when the meal is not served, I have had similar experiences on a smaller scale while "working the door" at the breakfast. The person at the door checks for tickets, determines the

1

number of seats available at a given moment, and decides how many people come inside to eat and how many remain outside waiting. In many ways the basement door is a joyful place — a place of handshakes and conversation and fellowship. However, the door also brings with it times of conflict and, almost always, a sense of failure and a glimpse of the cross.

The person working the door is the one who has to say, "No." "No, you can't come in yet. . . . I know it's 35 degrees and pouring down rain, but there's no room at the tables right now." "No, you can't use the bathroom right now. We're too busy." And, worst of all, "No, we're not serving breakfast anymore; you're too late." The scale is smaller than it was on the morning we did not serve breakfast at all, but the anger, frustration, and conflict are just as real. And the feelings of failure are much the same.

In Revelation 3:20 Jesus says, "Listen! I am standing at the door, knocking; if you hear my voice and open the door, I will come in to you and eat with you, and you with me." The person working the door at Butler Street is the one who often has to say "no" to that knock — "no" to the Jesus who comes to the door hungry or thirsty or naked. And, as Ron Jackson, a former member of the Open Door Community, commented, "It just breaks your heart."

For every "no," however, the person at the door gets to say "yes" dozens of times. Indeed, this "yes" is the larger context of every "no": "We're back. The grits and eggs, oranges and coffee are ready. Welcome!" This "yes," however, also has its cost. Even the "yes" is, in a profound sense, unfair, for it is spoken in the context of an unjust system that forces some people to live on the streets and wait in grit lines. Even the "yes" poignantly reminds me, in particular, that I am serving as yet another white, male "gatekeeper" for many poor African-Americans. Even the "yes" can break your heart, for it must be spoken face-to-face with poor, oppressed people. Each "yes" brings an encounter with the crucified Jesus, who comes to the door hungry and rejected.

Within this context, I heard the words of Micah: "What does Yahweh require of you but to do justice, and to love kindness, and to walk humbly with your God?" The order of these three demands, I realized, is important: justice, kindness, humility. In the process of seeking to do justice and love kindness, we are led to humility before God.

2

As we seek to be disciples of the poor, hungry, rejected Jesus, we encounter our sinfulness and our reliance on God's grace.

The basement door at Butler Street C.M.E. Church has brought this reality home to me time and again. I suspect I began volunteering at the breakfast in order to feel that I was doing some "good works," that I was being a more faithful disciple. I know I did not volunteer to have my heart broken. Ironically, however, at the basement door I have come not to greater confidence in my own "good works," but to a deeper awareness of my personal sins and my complicity in sinful systems, as well as to a greater dependence on the grace of Jesus Christ. What a revelation this has been! I had always assumed that discipleship *followed* the confession of sin and acceptance of forgiveness. The basement door, however, like the text from Micah, has taught me that this process is actually reversed: we do not fully know the depths of our sin and the reality of God's grace until we seek to follow the way of Jesus. Dietrich Bonhoeffer was right: grace is costly because it is inseparable from discipleship.[1] The basement door at Butler Street Church makes a person humble.

The text from Micah also forced me to think more deeply about justice and kindness in relation to the Butler Street Breakfast. On the morning we refused to serve breakfast to hungry people, our actions seemed to be anything but just and kind. On one level, we could only respond, "We have failed. We are sinners. Lord, have mercy upon us." At another level, however, Micah reminded me that the Butler Street Breakfast is not just about giving food, but about sharing meals. The purpose of the breakfast is not simply to throw food at hungry people as if they were animals. Rather, the purpose is to share meals together, day after day, which requires some order. Providing a peaceful meal for homeless people, I realized, is a greater act of kindness than slopping food on a tray in the midst of chaos. Similarly, treating people as responsible human beings and inviting them to come to the table with dignity is an important way of doing justice. For when people sit together at table in peace and dignity, God's shalom begins to become a reality.

When the goal is meal fellowship, sometimes food won't be

---

1. See Dietrich Bonhoeffer, *The Cost of Discipleship,* trans. R. H. Fuller, rev. ed. (New York: Macmillan, 1959).

served. To be sure, confession is required whenever the grits are returned to the Open Door, just as confession is necessary each day at the basement door. However, in the midst of failure, humbled before God, we are reminded by Micah of our purpose and our hope.[2]

Conversions in Context: A Road Map

The material in this book documents conversions in process — our own. Everything in these essays and sermons arises from our encounters with people who live on the streets of Atlanta, Georgia, and our involvement with the Open Door Community, an intentional Christian community modeled after the Catholic Worker Houses begun by Dorothy Day and deeply influenced by Koinonia Partners in Americus, Georgia, founded by Clarence and Florence Jordan.[1] Living and pursuing our vocations between the urban context of the Open Door and the quiet, upscale, suburban neighborhood surrounding Columbia Seminary (both of us live in seminary housing) keeps us in a constant, often uncomfortable state of tension, as "Sin, Grace, and the Basement Door" suggests. In many ways, our lives are representative of the tensions in which many mainstream Protestant congregations now find themselves. We are comfortable, segregated, suburban people, yet aware of desperate human needs just around the corner, needs that we know are somehow related to our comfortable, segregated, suburban lifestyles. These tensions bubble under the surface, and sometimes emerge into visibility, in the sermons and occasional essays that comprise this book.

While both of us spend most of our hours teaching at Columbia Seminary in Decatur, Georgia, each of us has found in the Open Door another vocational home. Over the past four years we have participated

---

1. Several years ago, Koinonia ceased being an intentional community.

in most of the ministries of the Open Door Community. In addition, guided by Ed Loring, a founding partner of the Open Door, we have spent hundreds of hours on the streets of Atlanta talking with homeless people, eating with them in soup kitchens, sleeping with them on sidewalks, worshiping with them in public spaces, and visiting them in the hospital and jails. We have also team-taught seminary courses on the streets with Ed. Chuck and Ed's course, "Good News to the Poor," has given students an opportunity to engage Scripture and practice preaching on the streets, while Stan and Ed's class, "Love Your Enemies: Hospitality and Solidarity in the New Testament and in Urban Atlanta," has focused on street-based exegesis of the key texts pertaining to our themes. Currently, both of us volunteer regularly at the Open Door, and Stan and his family are members of the worshiping community. Stan's wife Brenda serves as the Open Door's volunteer coordinator.

Because the material in this book originated in connection with the Open Door Community and downtown Atlanta, we need to lay some groundwork by describing some of the settings and institutions, mentioned repeatedly throughout the book, in which our conversions have taken place. These are, in our experience, "contested spaces" where "the reign of God" and "the powers and principalities" most clearly struggle for human lives and imaginations. We begin our descriptions with the Open Door Community itself. Then, following a brief look at Atlanta, we describe some of the key spaces in which the Open Door's ministry and our experiences have taken shape. These include the labor pools, Butler Street C.M.E. Church and the Butler Street Breakfast, Grady Memorial Hospital, and Woodruff Park.

The Open Door Community

Since 1981, the Open Door Community has been one of the loudest voices speaking on behalf of Atlanta's poorest and most vulnerable citizens. The Open Door, or "910" (its street address on Ponce de Leon Avenue) as it is known on the streets of Atlanta, is a residential Christian community consisting of twenty-five to thirty people (with a stable core of fifteen to twenty) who live together in a three-story, residential building that once housed the Women's Union Mission. The Open Door is a partnership ministry of the Presbytery of Greater Atlanta, but draws volunteers and financial support from individuals and congregations all over the world. The members of the community share in work, study, worship, and recreation. They are black and white, young and old; they are, or have been, teachers, students, pastors, military personnel, rich and poor, middle class and formerly homeless.

The Open Door's roots lie in the vision of two couples, Ed Loring and Murphy Davis, both ordained Presbyterian ministers, and Rob and Carolyn Johnson.[2] In 1975 Ed and Murphy began a ministry with the Clifton Presbyterian Church near downtown Atlanta. Shortly afterward, Rob and Carolyn joined the church. In this setting the four quickly became aware of a growing homeless population in the city. At the urging of homeless advocate Mitch Snyder, of the Community for Creative Nonviolence in Washington, D.C., Clifton Presbyterian Church opened the first free night shelter for homeless men in Atlanta in November, 1979. The Open Door evolved from this ministry and first opened its doors for a Christmas Day meal in 1981.[3]

Through their common life and work, the Open Door seeks, in Nicholas Lash's words, to "perform the Scriptures" in the urban context.[4] According to Lash, Christian Scripture is like the text of a drama or a musical score; its interpretation requires *performance*. That is, the Christian community's interpretation of Scripture is similar to the interpretation of a Shakespearean play by a company of actors or the interpretation of a Beethoven symphony by a group of musicians. The primary poles in biblical interpretation, Lash writes, are patterns of human action: on the one hand, "what was said and done and suffered, then, by Jesus and his disciples," and on the other, "what is said and done and suffered, now, by those who seek to share his obedience and hope."[5] As Lash concludes, ". . . the fundamental form of the Christian interpretation of Scripture is the life, activity, and organization of the believing community."[6]

2. Rob and Carolyn Johnson left the community in 1986.

3. For a more detailed account of the Open Door Community, see Peter R. Gathje, *Christ Comes in the Stranger's Guise: A History of the Open Door Community* (Atlanta: Open Door Community, 1991).

4. Nicholas Lash, "Performing the Scriptures," in *Theology on the Way to Emmaus* (London: SCM Press, 1986), pp. 37-46.

5. Lash, "Performing the Scriptures," p. 42.

6. Lash, "Performing the Scriptures," p. 42.

In the common life and work of the Open Door Community, we have discovered the truth of Lash's words. In this community we have discerned a virtuoso performance of Christian Scripture, and we have been blessed by the small roles we have been given among the Open Door's company of actors. All of the words that follow are merely footnotes to this community's primary performance of Scripture; our reflections grow out of this performance and seek to point back to it.

In their "performance of Scripture," The Open Door Community serves breakfast six days a week (ca. 65,000 breakfasts per year), offers soup kitchen four days a week (ca. 30,000 lunches each year), and offers showers and a change of clothing to Atlanta's homeless three days a week. Twenty-four hours a day the community provides fresh water for drinking and washing. From 9:00 A.M. until 8:30 P.M. each day the community offers other services, including the use of telephones, over-the-counter medicines, referrals, mail delivery to those who have no other address, blankets, and — a crucial service in a city with few public restrooms — bathroom facilities. On a typical night, between twenty-five and forty homeless people may sleep on the ground in the yard adjacent to the house. In addition to these ministries of compassion, the community engages in public advocacy on behalf of homeless people. Affordable housing, public toilets, and medical care are just a few of the issues the community has addressed publicly in recent years.

Another dimension of the community's ministry is expressed through the "Southern Prison Ministry," founded by Murphy Davis in 1977. Each month the Open Door provides transportation for as many as seventy-five family members who travel to visit inmates at the several prisons clustered in Hardwick, Georgia. The community also advocates for the abolition of the death penalty, for alternatives to prison, and for the rights and dignity of the growing numbers of women and men housed in this nation's prisons.

The other significant ministry of the Open Door involves education. The community hosts college, graduate, and seminary students in residential internships, as well as church and school groups who visit the community for days and sometimes weeks of work and learning. Each month the community publishes an internationally read newspaper, *Hospitality*, which offers a prophetic word on critical issues in Atlanta and around the world.

Through all of these ministries the Open Door seeks to be a voice for those who have no voice and to establish both a sanctuary and representative presence for those persons the business community and city leaders would prefer to sweep from view. In other words, through word, presence, and action, the Open Door seeks to reclaim human space and build relationships with and on behalf of the poor. Thus, hospitality, sanctuary (the maintenance of safe space), discernment, and solidarity with poor people, homeless people, and prisoners are the primary gifts and disciplines that mark the distinctive spirituality of this community. All of these gifts and disciplines are grounded in worship and coalesce around the quest to discern and live into the "Beloved Community."

Worship is not only central to the life of the Open Door, but also a key aspect of its presence in the city of Atlanta. Every day the community worships together, and each Sunday evening they celebrate the Eucharist. In addition, the Open Door regularly takes its worship onto the streets of the city. At least twice a year, during Holy Week and again in September during the "Festival of Shelters," members of the Open Door Community gather for "street worship" in key public spaces: in Woodruff Park (adjacent to the downtown business district); outside City Hall and the City Jail; in the plaza outside Grady, the city's public hospital; on the steps in front of the State Capitol; and outside the city shelter. These worship settings are chosen so as to lay claim to the presence of God in places where the powers of the world evidently reign and continue to crucify Jesus. By naming and giving thanks to God and by proclaiming Jesus as Lord in these spaces, the community seeks to disrupt business as usual.

During Holy Week and the Festival of Shelters, members of the community and other volunteers also participate in week-long street vigils, with different groups going out for twenty-four-hour periods throughout the week. When we have offered our classes with the Open Door, a twenty-four-hour street tour is always required, and usually is the most important learning experience in the course. The street tours serve two functions. First, they offer people like us, who live in the suburbs and attend relatively comfortable churches, a chance to walk where Atlanta's poor and homeless walk, eat what they eat, sleep where they sleep, and see what they see. In a small way, we begin to learn first-hand what life on the streets is like. Second, the

street tours provide an occasion — if only temporary — for participants to express solidarity with those we meet. Of course, we always
return to our comfortable homes and beds the next day, while those
with whom we have shared space on the streets continue their struggle just to survive. But twenty-four hours on the streets is nonetheless
for many people the beginning point both for discernment and for
more enduring expressions of solidarity and justice.

Amidst the touring, we hear the stories of homeless people and
prisoners, make new friends, and observe an array of urban characters
— pimps and prostitutes, hawkers and shoppers, tourists, dealers, police, street preachers, business people, bag ladies, and bounty hunters.
While many of us are visiting places we have been before, we nonetheless see and experience the city at a different angle and with different
eyes. A new type and level of discernment begins to emerge. By the end
of the day, as we make our way back toward the Open Door, we have begun to move from being merely voyeurs. We are starting to feel in our
bones the realities of poverty, homelessness, and the streets. The street
tour is not merely a challenging and distinctive educational experience.
For many of us it has become a foundational spiritual discipline, regularly repeated. For the first time in our lives we have really seen the city
where we live. And most astonishing of all, in the stranger by the dumpster we have seen the face of Christ in the midst of the city.

Atlanta: A View from the Streets[7]

The phoenix — the mythical bird that burns itself every five hundred
years and then rises rejuvenated from its own ashes — is for many

7. Although this book is not primarily about Atlanta, the city has been the
context of our experiences among the homeless. At least a brief look at Atlanta is
therefore required. As will be evident in what follows, we are not writing a tourist
brochure. While the city of Atlanta has many wonderful attributes, our focus here
is on those realities, particularly poverty and race, that have the greatest impact on
the people who live on the streets. Several written sources have been especially
useful in helping us to understand the particulars of the Atlanta story. First, Gary
Orfield and Carole Ashkinaze's 1991 book, *The Closing Door: Conservative Policy and
Black Opportunity* (Chicago: University of Chicago Press, 1991), provides an excel-
lent overview of what has happened in Atlanta during the last three decades with

Atlantans the appropriate symbol for the city. The image of fire recalls Atlanta's destruction during William Tecumseh Sherman's March to the Sea. Atlanta has indeed rebuilt itself and now projects images of dynamism and transformation. It has the fastest average speed on its highways of any major metropolitan American city, more "eye-in-the-sky" traffic helicopters than anywhere else in the nation, and more billboards per capita than anywhere else in the world.[8] It is the capital of the new South. Another phrase often used to describe Atlanta, "The City Too Busy to Hate," captures something of the quest for industrial development and expansion that has driven the city. This phrase also points to the reputation Atlanta has enjoyed throughout the United States, and perhaps even internationally, as a southern city that has made great strides in dealing with racial issues. These images comprise central elements of Atlanta's popular mythology and have shaped the city's pervasive "boosterism" through the years.[9]

---

regard to race, economics, and education. By this means they are also able to offer a compelling critical analysis of the effects of the social policies that have dominated throughout the nation during this period. While much of the data in the book is nearly ten years old, the picture it provides remains essentially accurate, except that the continuing boom during the 1990s "reached a little deeper" (noted in electronic correspondence between Saunders and Prof. Orfield). Second, Charles Rutheiser's *Imagineering Atlanta: The Politics of Place in the City of Dreams* (New York: Verso, 1996) combines anthropology and history with political and geographical analyses to produce an illuminating — and scathing — perspective on Atlanta's growth. Third, Clarence N. Stone's now classic study, *Regime Politics: Governing Atlanta, 1946-1988* (Lawrence, Kansas: The University Press of Kansas, 1989), provides a detailed, multifaceted discussion and analysis of Atlanta's political and economic powers since World War II. In addition, we have benefited from access to a variety of up-to-the-moment statistical analyses gathered by the staff at Atlanta's Task Force for the Homeless. Holly Levenson of the Atlanta Labor Pool Workers' Union graciously shared their report entitled "Atlanta's Hardest Working People: A Report on Day Labor Pools in Metro Atlanta," which summarizes research conducted between 1995 and 1998 by students at Atlanta area colleges and universities, working in conjunction with the Union.

8. Rutheiser, *Imagineering Atlanta*, pp. 111, 113.

9. On Atlanta's obsession with "image," John Lewis, the U.S. Representative from Atlanta and a leading figure in the civil rights movement, has stated, "The city of Atlanta is very image-conscious. There [is] a great [deal] of pride, but we want to protect our community. We don't want any blemishes to come out into the public, and the business community is probably more sensitive than any other segment" (*Chicago Tribune,* 20 November 1988; cited in Orfield and Ashkinaze, *The Closing Door,*

Myth both reveals and hides reality. And that is certainly the case for Atlanta's economic and racial myths. For many years, without a doubt, Atlanta has been "on the move." Atlanta's rapid, dynamic growth as a major, international city has been real — culminating, for many people, in the summer of 1996, when the city hosted the Centennial Olympic Games. Atlanta's "progress," however, has come at a high human cost. Over the last fifty years Atlanta's development of transportation, commercial, and entertainment venues (including Olympic sites) has displaced some 100,000 residents of areas in and adjacent to the central business districts. In the wake of this "urban renewal" and development, once vital black neighborhoods such as Buttermilk Bottom, and parts of Vine City, Summerhill, Mechanicsville, and Peoplestown, saw their low-income housing stock destroyed and their neighborhoods and community life decimated. Most of the people displaced in these purges were left to their own devices to find affordable housing. Often they found none at all.

In addition, as we write this, Atlanta is just beginning to grapple with the environmental consequences of its long-term orientation toward "progress" and expansion, which has created massive traffic congestion and seriously degraded regional air quality, engendering comparisons with Los Angeles. Air quality alerts, which warn of dangerous levels of smog in the city, are now a daily part of life at certain times of the year.[10] Atlanta's rise from the ashes appears to have created more "smoke" than did General Sherman.

Smoke also envelops the racial aspects of Atlanta's image, which are complicated at best. Over the years, to be sure, a kind of truce was built up between black and white leaders in Atlanta, and the city definitely projected an "image as a hospitable place of racial moderation."[11] In some ways this image has been the reality. During the sixties, for example, the "racial détente" that had been established in the city held up amidst the racial fury of the decade. Unlike other major American cities,

---

p. 26). Atlanta's long-standing "boosterism" and image-management are detailed in Rutheiser, *Imagineering Atlanta*, pp. 12-73.

10. For a recent account of the problems created by Atlanta's rapid growth and development, see Daniel Pedersen, Vern E. Smith, and Jerry Adler, "Sprawling, Sprawling . . . ," *Newsweek*, July 19, 1999, pp. 22-27.

11. Gary M. Pomerantz, *Where Peachtree Meets Sweet Auburn: A Saga of Race and Family* (New York: Penguin Books, 1996), p. 19.

Atlanta did not burn again.[12] Today, Atlanta is often touted as a "black Mecca" in the national press. The population of Atlanta proper is predominantly black, and African-Americans have held the office of mayor continuously since the election of Maynard Jackson in 1973.

Despite these appearances, however, the city's projected image has often veiled stark realities behind it. Atlanta today remains among the most segregated cities in the nation, both racially and economically.[13] Geographically, the racial and economic realities of the city can be seen in the contrast between the wealthier, predominantly white, northern suburbs, where fewer than 6 percent live in poverty, and the poorer, predominantly black population located south of Ponce de Leon Avenue, where, in some areas, no more than 6 percent live above the poverty line.[14] While Atlanta's economic growth has surpassed that of the nation over the last three decades, the gaps between rich and poor, black and white, city and suburb have grown ever deeper, with more devastating results for poor families and individuals.[15] This

12. Pomerantz, *Where Peachtree Meets Sweet Auburn*, p. 19.

13. Rutheiser, *Imagineering Atlanta*, p. 86; also Orfield and Ashkinaze, *The Closing Door*, pp. 69-77.

14. Rutheiser, *Imagineering Atlanta*, p. 119. While many blacks have moved to the suburbs during Atlanta's economic boom over the last three decades, real estate lending policies have kept them mostly segregated in certain regions of the metropolitan area, where they continue to experience weaker schools and lesser services (Orfield and Ashkinaze, *The Closing Door*, pp. 25ff.).

15. In 1990, for example, the median income of white households in Atlanta proper was $61,691, compared to $22,372 for African-American households (Rutheiser, *Imagineering Atlanta*, p. 86). Segregation has powerful economic effects, isolating much of the black population, and especially the poorest people, from access to better paying jobs, which have grown dramatically in some (mostly white) suburbs, where MARTA, the regional public transit system, does not reach. Between 1980 and 1985 the five predominantly black regions of the city had a job growth rate of less than 5 percent, while the seven regions of metro Atlanta with greater than 90 percent white population had an average job growth rate more than fourteen times higher (Orfield and Ashkinaze, *The Closing Door*, p. 17). A 1997 study by Dr. Michael Rich of Emory University concludes that only one in three unfilled jobs in the Atlanta region pays more than minimum wage, is accessible by public transportation, and requires only entry-level skills (Atlanta Task Force for the Homeless, unpublished paper entitled "The Impact of Welfare Reform on Homelessness," p. 3). For a thorough discussion of these issues, see William Julius Wilson, *When Work Disappears: The World of the New Urban Poor* (New York: Alfred A. Knopf, 1996), especially pp. 3-86.

13

situation has led some people to describe Atlanta as a big doughnut, with a wealthy, white suburban population surrounding a "center city" that is predominantly black and devastatingly poor.[16]

The racial and economic politics of the city are likewise often obscured by the city's image. As was noted above, African-Americans make up the majority in the city and have held the position of mayor since 1973. However, this African-American majority and the succession of African-American mayors have learned that the path toward substantive change runs through the white-dominated coalition of

16. Over the last three decades the gaps between city and suburban and between black and white incomes have grown, and the gap between black and white rates of home ownership has also increased. Since 1970 the percentage of central Atlanta households in poverty has more than doubled, while housing costs have increased. In the most recent statistics available from Atlanta's Task Force for the Homeless, the average household calling the hotline seeking shelter was paying 70 percent of its income for rent. Between 1980 and 1990, the percentage of African-American households in poverty in Atlanta nearly doubled to more than one-third of all households. As Atlanta-based urban anthropologist Charles Rutheiser concludes, "By any and every statistical measure, from poverty and unemployment to graduation rates and crime, the quality of life 'enjoyed' by the city's African-American majority plummeted during this period" (p. 63).

The future also does not look bright for Atlanta's poor and black population. Since 1980, college access, the key to economic viability in this society, has grown for whites, but diminished sharply for blacks in Atlanta, even though more blacks are graduating from high school (Orfield and Ashkinaze, *The Closing Door*, pp. 103-73). The breakdown of the educational system for African-Americans means that more workers will be competing for an ever-dwindling number of low-skill jobs, many of which do not even pay an adequate wage.

One of the effects of welfare reform enacted in 1996 has been to push even more people into the pool of workers who are competing for a limited number of jobs that do not pay enough to buy food, housing, and medical care. (See Katherine S. Newman, *No Shame in My Game: The Working Poor in the Inner City* [New York: Alfred A. Knopf and the Russell Sage Foundation, 1999], especially pp. 56-60.) The greatest impact of welfare reform has been on single mothers. In 1997, 61 percent of those who appealed to the Task Force for the Homeless for assistance in Atlanta were women; 47 percent were women with children.

During the next decade cities like Atlanta will also have to absorb increasing numbers of released prisoners — the inevitable outcome of our current rush to incarcerate more and more people. These people, mostly young black men, will emerge from their incarceration without job skills (prison job-training programs have been sharply curtailed since the 1980s), without hope, and probably angry (Sasha Abramsky, "When They Get Out," *The Atlantic Monthly* [June 1999]: 30-36).

downtown business leaders, Central Atlanta Progress (CAP), which greatly limits the power of the city government.[17] In addition, because much of metro Atlanta's wealth lies outside the "city limits," the economic needs of the city proper are often held hostage to the wishes of residents of the outlying suburbs. While African-Americans may hold the political offices, white Atlantans usually hold the economic strings. City officials consequently often lack not only the power, but also the resources to address the city's problems.

One of these problems, a direct consequence of the city's racial and economic realities, is homelessness. Although numerical estimates of homeless people are notoriously difficult to develop,[18] careful studies by Atlanta's Task Force for the Homeless suggest that on any given night between 11,500 and 16,000 people are homeless in the city.[19] In

17. See Stone, *Regime Politics,* which provides a detailed analysis of the relationship between the city's government and business interests.

18. On the difficulties in "counting" homeless people, see Joel Blau, *The Visible Poor: Homelessness in the United States* (New York: Oxford University Press, 1992; Oxford paperback, 1993), pp. 15-30. Blau's book is one of the most helpful books on homelessness in the United States.

19. The latest statistics available to us (through the Atlanta Task Force for the Homeless) represent the state of homelessness in Atlanta between 1996 and 1998. Recognizing the difficulties associated with counting homeless people, the Task Force uses two methods of counting — "annual" (the number of people homeless in the course of a year) and "point in time" (the number of people homeless on a given night) — and works toward "high" and "low" estimates rather than a single figure. Their "low" annual estimate of homelessness in Atlanta is 45,877 persons; the "high" figure is 63,080. Point in time analyses indicate that between 11,469 and 15,770 people were homeless on any given day or night.

Homelessness in Atlanta is growing due to a number of factors. First among these is a persistent decline in the number of affordable housing units. In 1996, the difference between the number of low-income renters (97,000) and the units of low-income housing available (49,000) was 48,000, up from 46,300 in 1991. Second, welfare reform continues to add to this number, due especially to the increase in women and children who have lost all welfare benefits. Third, between 1996 and 1998, Atlanta lost nearly one-third of its available shelter beds — a drop from 2,386 in 1996 to 1,349 beds at the time of the last available survey. During the last decade demolition and price gentrification of low-income housing has produced a loss of about 5,000 very low-income units, which were formerly available primarily for very low-income women and children.

The 1997 homeless population in Atlanta included: Women with Children, 47 percent; Single Men, 24 percent; Single Women, 14 percent; Couples with

response to this grim reality, Atlanta has followed the path of many other major cities. Rather than seeking solutions to the underlying causes of homelessness, the city has responded by enacting policies that penalize homeless people and seek to drive them off the streets. Atlanta's "Urban Camping" ordinance, for example, which targets homeless people, effectively criminalizes poverty by making it illegal for anyone to lie on the ground to rest in a public place.[20] In addition, homeless people are particularly vulnerable to Atlanta's concern about its image. When major events come to town, whether it's the Democratic National Convention, the Super Bowl, or the Olympics, Atlanta's homeless are "swept" off the streets and out of sight, whether into jails or to other parts of the city. Before the Olympics, many homeless people joked that the new city jail would be *their* "Olympic housing."

Atlanta's economic and racial myths thus both reveal and hide reality. Atlanta can be a stimulating place for a white, middle-class seminary professor. From the perspective of a poor, African-American homeless person, however, the city takes on a very different, more threatening appearance. This "other Atlanta," the one seen from the streets, has been the context of our conversions.

Children, 11 percent; Couples without Children, 3 percent; Men with Children, 1 percent. Up to 33 percent of the adult homeless population have a serious mental illness. Approximately 50 percent have a current or past alcohol or drug abuse problem. Of those surveyed, 37 percent had been homeless for less than 3 months, 29 percent for 4-12 months, 15 percent for 13-24 months, 9 percent for 25-48 months, and 10 percent for more than 4 years.

20. *Code of Ordinances of the City of Atlanta,* 106-12. The language of the ordinance allows for broad interpretation and enforcement. In July of 1999, after we had mailed our manuscript to the publisher, the city of Atlanta settled a federal lawsuit that the ACLU had filed in 1997 against the Urban Camping Ordinance. Because the law targeted homeless people and essentially made being a homeless person a crime, the ACLU had argued that the law violated the equal protection clause of the Fourteenth Amendment to the U.S. Constitution. In the settlement, the city of Atlanta adopted a new urban camping law that allows police to make arrests only if it appears that a public space is being used "for private living accommodations" (e.g., regular cooking, erection of structures, storage of personal property for long periods of time). The city also agreed to pay $28,000 to the nine homeless people who were plaintiffs in the suit and $58,000 in legal fees. It remains to be seen how this change in the "letter of the law" will affect the actual treatment of homeless people in the city.

Contested Spaces

Labor Pools[21]

Some of the most pernicious spaces in which poor people experience the city are the labor pools, which epitomize an economic system that enriches the few by enslaving the poor. Few people in the middle class even know that the "pools" exist and that they are proliferating. Part of a growing national trend toward the elimination of full-time jobs with benefits in favor of temporary or part-time work,[22] labor pools are the heart of a system — including bunkhouses, shelters, liquor stores, and the illegal drug industry — that feeds on poor people. They are one expression within our own country of the international movement Kevin Bales calls "the new slavery."[23] As of 1998, the city of Atlanta proper had approximately fifteen licensed and ten unlicensed labor pools, and the metropolitan area had approximately sixty, employing about five thousand people per day. Dallas and Atlanta lead the nation in the number of day labor pools.

As Bales notes in his description of the new slavery developing in the global economy, poverty and social dislocation are the key factors that make people vulnerable to enslavement. This is true here in the United States just as much as it is in other parts of the world. Homelessness, the disruption of families (especially among the poor), the shredding of the social safety net once associated with welfare and Medicaid, the growth of low-paying jobs that provide no benefits, the flood of people with minimal education and skills seeking to enter the workforce, and the physical isolation of the poor from the sight of the more affluent have combined to create just the right conditions for exploitation and enslavement. The men and women we have encountered on Atlanta's streets are just the leading edge of a population seg-

21. For most of the data in this section we depend on the report compiled by the Atlanta Labor Pool Workers' Union entitled "Atlanta's Hardest Working People: A Report on Day Labor Pools in Metro Atlanta."

22. Lawrence Mishel, Jared Bernstein, John Schmitt, *The State of Working America, 1998-1999* (Ithaca, New York: ILR Press/Cornell University Press, 1999), pp. 242-53.

23. Kevin Bales, *Disposable People: New Slavery in the Global Economy* (Berkeley: University of California Press, 1999).

ment that will explode in the coming years, victims of the demonic side of our economy.

Although middle-class stereotypes depict homeless persons as winos and addicts, a growing number of homeless people in this country work at least eight hours a day, often in difficult, dangerous, physically and mentally exhausting, but menial circumstances.[24] Among the people we have gotten to know through the ministries of the Open Door Community, a common pattern can be observed: some personal crisis such as sickness or divorce, or a more general trend such as industrial relocation or "downsizing," leads to the loss of "living-wage" work. Single parents, especially women with small children, are particularly vulnerable since welfare reform. Savings are quickly drained, and one can find oneself on the streets in a matter of days. Sometimes this crisis is exacerbated by denial — a "this can't be happening to me" reaction that combines anger and passivity. Unless the person has other skills, personal contacts, or family resources to draw upon, it is very difficult to get back up from the deepening sinkhole.

The toll of even a few days on the streets can be debilitating. Living on the streets rapidly drains one's energy. Health risks in general are much higher on the streets, and adequate health care is less available and must be paid for at the expense of housing or food. The psychic toll may be even heavier; while it may be true that "absolute power tends to corrupt absolutely," nothing is more corrosive to the human spirit than powerlessness.[25] Mental illness is often as much an effect as a cause of homelessness.[26]

The only direct beneficiaries in this increasingly common scenario are the usually anonymous owners of the labor pools. Labor pools serve as "middle-men" between corporations and businesses seeking low-cost employees and workers desperate to find any kind of work they can. Labor pools save companies money in two ways. First, for companies that have fluctuating labor needs, it is cheaper to pay laborers on a day-to-day basis than to hire workers for the long term.

24. According to a 1997 survey of 29 cities by the U.S. Conference of Mayors, one in five homeless people is employed in full- or part-time work.

25. Thanks to Holly Levenson of the Atlanta Labor Pool Workers' Union for this observation.

26. Blau, *The Visible Poor*, pp. 77-90. Blau here offers a helpful analysis of the relationship between homelessness and mental illness.

Second, hiring workers through the pools means companies don't have to pay for insurance or benefits.

While most of us are unaware of the existence or character of labor pools — they are usually located in nondescript spaces and have little or no signage — we nonetheless come in contact every day with "products" produced by labor pool workers. The *Atlanta Journal-Constitution*, the major morning and evening newspaper for the Atlanta region, hires workers through the labor pools to assemble newspapers, especially the Sunday edition. Atlanta's large construction companies are also in the picture, though obscured. The subcontractors they often use to do the actual work typically rely on the labor pools to supply employees for all but the most specialized construction jobs. Most, if not all, of Atlanta's new Olympic venues were constructed using labor pool workers. Other labor pool employees find work as "black and whites" — waiters, waitresses, and service personnel for conventions. Several of the colleges and universities in Atlanta use labor pool employees for various jobs, especially on grounds-keeping and maintenance crews. Moving companies, the "hospitality" industry (hotels), and country clubs round out the primary group of businesses that rely daily on labor pool workers.

Labor pools hire workers on a day-to-day basis. The typical worker who depends on Atlanta's downtown labor pools for employment is an African-American male, usually homeless. Labor pools often specialize in offering certain ethnic types of employees, however, so that Asian workers can be found at one pool, Latino workers at another, African-Americans at another. Jobless women seek work through the labor pools much less frequently than do men; for women the labor market is located around AFDC (Aid for Families and Dependent Children) offices.[27] The ethnic/gender specializations of the various labor pools thus offer another advantage to many companies by allowing them to bypass hiring laws that restrict racial or gender discrimination.

Labor pool workers typically share other common traits beyond ethnicity. Most did not receive an adequate high school education, went from high school to the military, from the military to a job in

27. Since welfare reform, AFDC offices have been redesignated "TANF" — Temporary Assistance for Needy Families — but "AFDC" has persisted in common parlance.

manufacturing, but lost that job through "downsizing." Many labor pool employees also have some kind of criminal record, which is an obstacle to permanent employment. Many are also trying to support children or families from whom they are separated.

A day in the life of a labor pool worker might go something like this. If the worker, who is often homeless, has found space to sleep at a night shelter or a bunkhouse, he will typically ask for an early wake-up call, usually around 4:00 or 4:30 A.M., so that he can make it to the labor pool by 5:00 A.M. The "bunkhouses" are often located adjacent to the labor pools and may be owned by the same company. Bunkhouses offer warehouse-style accommodations — for example, fifty cots lined up in a large room — for approximately $7-$10 per night. Many homeless workers actually prefer the "safety" of the streets to the conditions of the bunkhouses.

After making it to the labor pool and getting on a list, many workers will wait in or around the labor pool until 8:00 A.M. to get a "ticket," i.e., a job assignment. About a third of those waiting for work do not find any. There is no opportunity for breakfast, and lunches supplied (or sold) by the labor pools are minimal — cheese sandwiches, for example. The labor pool system of employment in effect forces people to choose between food and work; deciding to work means that one will not be able to get food at the soup kitchens open during the day.

Labor pool spaces are typically dirty and dark, with simple benches or folding chairs for those who await a call. Bathrooms are filthy if they are available at all. Workers are not paid for the time they spend waiting in the labor pool for a job, nor for the time (often substantial) spent in transit to and from a work site. In the suburbs and around housing projects one may also encounter "unincorporated" pools, located outdoors, around bus stops, for example, where large numbers of men, usually from the same ethnic group, congregate early in the morning.

Although the labor pool receives $10-$15 per hour for each worker, the workers themselves are paid minimum wage.[28] The labor pools keep the difference. They also make deductions, often illegal,

---

28. The minimum wage was $4.75 per hour during the time a study of Atlanta labor pools was conducted (1995-1998).

from workers' paychecks — for transportation costs, safety equipment, and food, in addition to taxes — with the result that the worker usually takes home $25-$30 for eight hours of work (but twelve hours or more of travail). Many times, the taxes and social security payments deducted from a worker's check are never actually paid to the government.

Although it is illegal, some labor pools pay workers by vouchers rather than by check. The vouchers can be cashed only at designated liquor stores, where drug dealers also can be found. Transportation to and from the store will further deplete the worker's cash-in-hand at the end of the day. Those who choose to walk rather than pay for the transportation supplied by the labor pool run a greater risk of being robbed, since thieves prowl the route between the labor pool and the liquor store. Whatever income remains goes for bunkhouse costs (and thus back into the hands of the labor pool owners), for a meal, or sometimes for alcohol or drugs. Those who would dare to challenge this system at any point are merely dismissed without pay, for there are plenty of others willing to step in to take their places.

Butler Street Breakfast

Just a few blocks south and east of the heart of downtown Atlanta, and a few blocks from "Sweet Auburn" (once the center of African-American culture and business in Atlanta) is an area where the Open Door has been contesting space with the powers in Atlanta for nearly two decades. Grady Memorial Hospital, the large public health care facility that serves Atlanta's poor and many others in need of state-of-the-art care, dominates the area. Within the blocks immediately adjacent to the hospital, one can also find Butler Street Christian Methodist Episcopal Church, the city morgue, Hugh Spalding Children's Hospital, the Municipal Market, Grady Homes (one of Atlanta's housing projects), and the edges of the Georgia State University campus.

When Ed Loring began to explore this area during the early eighties, several labor pools could also be found. One day Ed asked Alvin Dollar, then the director of the City Day Labor Center, what the men who came to the Center for work most needed. Alvin's answer was no small surprise. "Breakfast. The men and women who leave the

Labor Center for work have to go without food. The choice is between food and work." This is the daily reality for the urban poor all across this country.

As a result of this conversation, the Open Door began offering breakfasts out of the Labor Center in December, 1982, at first just once a week. When city officials put a stop to the breakfast, claiming that the Labor Center was a place for people to get jobs, not eat, the meal was moved to the streets, and shortly thereafter to the basement of nearby Butler Street C.M.E. Church, which stands at the corner of Butler Street and Coca-Cola Place, within a block of the main entrance to Grady Hospital. The Open Door served breakfast — an egg, cheese grits, orange slices, coffee, and a vitamin — five days a week from the end of January, 1983, until the end of September, 1998, when the church's pastor moved the congregation "in a new direction."[29]

The Butler Street Breakfast was always a wonderful combination of hospitality (offered both to and by the guests), joy, rest, warmth, and friendliness, punctuated by tension, occasional bursts of violence, and the daily frustrations of having to say "no" to some would-be guests. During the years of its operation, the Butler Street Breakfast also served as a point of engagement, action, and reflection — i.e., a "contested space" — for numerous students from Emory's Candler School of Theology, the Interdenominational Theological Center, and especially Columbia Seminary. In the reflection time that followed breakfast each day, and in our time after that on the streets, we learned to read Scripture and preach in a context much different from what most of us know on Sunday mornings. The ending of the Butler Street Breakfast in 1998 represents in our mind one place where the powers devoted to image and "progress" finally won — at least for now. The contest continues down the street at Grady Memorial Hospital.

29. At the time the Butler Street Breakfast ended, the Open Door was serving up to 250 men, women, and children each morning. Unable to secure another location in the Grady Hospital area, the Open Door now serves the breakfast from its "home" at 910 Ponce de Leon Ave.

Grady Memorial Hospital

Grady Hospital first opened in May, 1892, to offer health care to Atlanta's poorest citizens; the original facility had ten beds for paying patients and one hundred charity beds. Since 1946, a public commission
established by Fulton and Dekalb counties has governed the hospital,
which is still charged with providing health care services to the uninsured and under-insured. Today Grady is a 953-bed hospital with an internationally recognized trauma center. It functions as a teaching hospital for the schools of medicine at Emory University and Morehouse
College. Grady's patient base, which is 85 percent African-American, is
made up predominantly of the people living in Atlanta's urban, inner-
city environment, 73 percent of whom are African-Americans. Over half
of the uninsured and under-insured households that use Grady Hospital are employed full-time.

In the halls of Grady, Atlanta's poor continue to struggle for life.
They wait in endless lines for services and medications, paying with
their time. They grow frustrated with the bureaucracy. But the primary
threat to their lives — the economic and political powers that would
restrict care to paying customers, or shut the hospital altogether —
continues to contest this space, though out of public sight most of the
time. During the last several years, Grady Hospital, like many public
hospitals across the country, has been under increasing financial pressure. This pressure has come first from politicians based in northern
Fulton County, who see it as a drain on their tax dollars. Still more recently the Balanced Budget Act of 1997, the decrease in federal fund-
ing associated with welfare reform, and the reduction in the number of
people eligible for Medicaid, has forced the hospital to find new ways
to make ends meet.

In response to this financial crisis, Grady in 1999 proposed raising the co-pay for prescriptions from fifty cents to ten dollars for its
poorest patients, thereby putting more economic pressure on those
least able to handle it. To people in the middle class, ten dollars doesn't
seem like a lot, but for those who live on the streets or spend all of their
fixed income on rent and food, such an increase effectively places
medical care beyond their reach. For many, whose lives depend on
their medication, such a policy is a prescription for death. In response
to this situation, members of the Open Door Community, Concerned

Black Clergy, and other activist groups have participated in a number of political actions, including civil disobedience, aimed at protecting the availability of health care for the poorest people in Atlanta. At the time of this writing, the issue has not yet been resolved.[30]

Woodruff Park

Few places in Atlanta better symbolize the powers' efforts to contest and control space than Woodruff Park, a four-acre parcel of land on Peachtree Street in the heart of downtown Atlanta. Across Peachtree Street to the north stands the charcoal-colored box that is the Equitable Tower. Further south looms the edgy, imposing Georgia Pacific building. To the immediate east stands a tall, nondescript building now identified with a large banking firm. The site is two blocks north of the Five-Points MARTA (Metropolitan Atlanta Regional Transit Authority) station where the East-West and North-South lines of the city's commuter rail system meet, and "Underground Atlanta," the city's floundering commercial attempt to draw visitors into the area.

Coca-Cola President Robert Woodruff purchased the land for the park anonymously in 1971 and donated it to the city. The park opened in 1973 as "Central City Park," and quickly attracted a mixed clientele of daytime office workers and poor and homeless people. A 1980 renovation focused the park's activity on a large, central plaza surrounded by trees. During the 1980s the migration of downtown businesses and workers to other parts of the city altered the mix of users, creating an impression that the area had been taken over by the homeless and was no longer safe. Ironically, however, as Charles Rutheiser observes, although petty theft and aggressive panhandling were problems, it was the homeless people themselves who were most at risk in the park. Between 1992 and 1993, thirteen deaths occurred in the park, most due to exposure during the winter.[31] During the day, and especially during the lunch hour, the vast majority of users were office workers and stu-

30. For a discussion of the situation at Grady Hospital as a microcosm of the larger health care crisis in the United States, see Neil Shulman, "Prescription Protest," *The Nation,* August 9/16, 1999, pp. 24-27.

31. Rutheiser, *Imagineering Atlanta,* p. 212.

dents and faculty from Georgia State University, who commingled with homeless people, usually without incident. Street preachers, artists, martial artists, and vendors added to the mix, creating something approximating an "authentically diverse urban space,"[32] or at least as close as one can come to that in Atlanta.

In the early 1990s the city implemented a series of ordinances focused on panhandling and "urban camping," to go along with existing ordinances against public urination (even in discreet places, such as in an alley or behind a dumpster), all of which were aimed at driving homeless people from the area. Mounted police would sometimes position their horses over homeless persons sleeping in the park, terrorizing the waking offender, who risked being trampled. In September and October, 1993, twelve members of the Open Door were arrested and jailed for "slouching," or lying on benches in Woodruff Park, generating public awareness that led the city eventually to suspend the law. But in 1994 the city closed the park for a five-million-dollar face-lift, ostensibly to upgrade the "public character" of the area in preparation for the Olympics. The designers of the new park were called specifically to create a space that would be inhospitable to homeless people. The new space included fewer benches, which were placed end to end around the edge of the park, making interaction with others difficult. Each bench also came equipped with armrests spaced a few feet apart, making it almost impossible for anyone to lie down. Automatic sprinklers in the grass made certain that no one would stay on the lawn for long. After its completion, the mayor pronounced the park "a beautiful place to look at," unintentionally admitting its implausibility as a place for folks to rest or interact.[33]

When Woodruff Park reopened late in 1995, the Open Door Community and more than two hundred of the city's homeless staged a public worship, reclaiming the park for all of Atlanta's citizens, especially the homeless. Today the park remains a contested space, still used in a limited way by homeless people — and by everyone else — and still the focus of police sweeps.

32. Rutheiser, *Imagineering Atlanta,* p. 212.
33. The city later added some bolted-down metal tables and chairs in one section of the park, which did allow for more interaction. Recently, however, these table and chairs were removed.

Street Themes

Since both of us are professors at a seminary, we necessarily have learned to engage our context in Atlanta through "theological" lenses. Anyone who studies theology for very long tends to develop a rather specialized vocabulary, made up of the terms that distinguish this discipline from others and that reflect the primary interests of its leading practitioners. Much of the theological and disciplinary language we have learned, and still use, in seminary loses its pertinence or rings hollow when we move to the streets. To speak there of "eschatology," "homiletics," "church growth," or "postmodern theology" is, of course, to invite misunderstanding, if not ridicule. We have learned that it's usually better just to listen and to stand with those in need.

When we sat down to look at what each of us had written over the last few years, we were mildly surprised to find the degree to which certain language shaped both of our reflections, despite our diverse disciplinary backgrounds. As may already be clear, the primary terms include "worship" (and "Word"), "discernment," "hospitality," "powers and principalities," and "solidarity," which are all aspects of "engaging the powers," or "contesting space" in the name of the God we know in Jesus Christ.[34] These are not terms one hears every day on the streets, to be sure, but they are the theological terms that have emerged as most useful in naming our experiences and practices. This terminology winds its way throughout this collection, gathering, we hope, richness and depth along the way. We have chosen four of these themes as the primary poles around which to organize the essays in this book: worship, Word, solidarity, and space.

34. The phrase "engaging the powers" is borrowed from Walter Wink, *Engaging the Powers* (Philadelphia: Fortress Press, 1992).

WORSHIP

I appeal to you therefore, brothers and sisters, by the mercies of God, to present your bodies as a living sacrifice, holy and acceptable to God, which is your spiritual worship. Do not be conformed to this world, but be transformed by the renewing of your minds, so that you may discern what is the will of God — what is good and acceptable and perfect.

ROMANS 12:1-2

Street Prayer

Woodcut; 22 ¾″ × 24 ¼″; © 1999 Christina Bray

Discernment on the Road to Emmaus

In the account of Jesus' appearance to two of his disciples on the road to Emmaus (Luke 24:13-35), the evangelist Luke presents us with a story that encapsulates some of the key tensions of the Christian tradition. Here we encounter Jesus crucified and raised, stranger and friend, human and divine. Perhaps the most disturbing element of the story, however, is the image of Jesus visible and then, suddenly, invisible. With this motif Luke takes us to the heart of the disciples' quest to discern the reality of the resurrection. Two thousand years of reflection about the resurrection has left us still searching for hard facts, for something we can prove on the world's terms. The Messiah has proved remarkably resilient and slippery through all of our attempts to secure his image, to catch him and contain him for even a moment. He remains ever just beyond the place where we can hold him in our gaze and grasp his image.

In the story of what transpired on the Emmaus road Luke weaves together these glimpses of the crucified and resurrected, visible and invisible Messiah with images of the worshiping community. The story has all the components of a good worship service: gathering, Scripture reading, story telling and proclamation, prayer, and finally Eucharist — all leading out into witness and mission. By weaving these elements together, Luke reminds us that the worshiping community has always been the place where disciples practice the disciplines of discernment and witness. Worship is the social space, in other words, where the church gathers to watch for and describe the presence of the resurrected Lord in its midst. And Easter in particular is the season when

29

we wash the dirt of the world from our collective corrective lenses, when the light of the resurrection shines into the darkened corners of our imaginations so that the glory of the Lord can be seen once again. Easter, in other words, is about seeing clearly.

The witness of both the evangelists and the apostle Paul is that the task of seeing clearly is an exceedingly difficult undertaking, one that requires constant practice. It also requires the cultivation of a peculiar form of imagination, which is the word we use to describe "how we see." Somewhere on the way to our modern, scientific worldview, imagination got a bad rap. It became the realm of fiction, especially of fantastic images and ideas divorced from the realities of everyday life. We now often think of imagination as something that children possess in abundance, and therefore as something that must be subdued in order to achieve "realistic," practical, and "down-to-earth" engagement with life. But this usually means coming to terms with the world's way of looking at things. Discipleship entails nurturing another way of seeing.

Our wariness with regard to the imagination can be deadly when it comes to the walk of Christian faith, which is guided by imagination rooted in the stories of Jesus and his disciples, especially in the story of Jesus' crucifixion and resurrection. Christians and churches that fail to nurture a "resurrection imagination" inevitably become blinded by the "realities" of this world, unable to discern God's life-giving presence in our life together and unable to sustain a faithful Christian witness. Easter is the season when we in the church have our vision tested. When we go looking for the risen Messiah, will he be visible, or will the images and imaginations of this world choke out his presence?

Over a century ago a British cleric, classicist, educator, and Shakespearean scholar named Edwin Abbott Abbott published a small volume exploring the world of perception and dimension. Abbott's work has remained popular among physicists and others in the scientific community because it serves as a wonderful introduction to the world of multiple dimensions. It deserves to be read by Christians, as well, for its capacity to illustrate what the struggle to establish and nurture a resurrection imagination is like. *Flatland: A Romance of Many Dimensions*[1] is set

1. Edwin Abbott Abbott, *Flatland: A Romance of Many Dimensions* (Princeton: Princeton University Press, 1991; reprint of the 6th edition, New York: Dover Publications, 1953).

in a world of two dimensions where everyone is a geometric object: women, who occupy the lowest rung in the social order, are mere lines; polygons make up the nobility; and circles are the High Priests. Flatland is an orderly, hierarchical, and relatively unchanging world. The chief character in the story is Mr. Square, a conservative member of the establishment, who unquestioningly accepts the sacred belief that reality consists of only two dimensions.

The story involves the events that transpire after Mr. Square is visited one day by the mysterious Lord Sphere. Although Lord Sphere is a three-dimensional entity, Mr. Square perceives him only as a circle that is able to change sizes, apparently by magic. When rational explanation fails to convince Mr. Square that a third dimension exists, Lord Sphere peels Mr. Square off of his two-dimensional world and leaves him to float about in Spaceland (the world of three dimensions), like a sheet of paper in the wind. Because Mr. Square is still able to perceive reality only in two dimensions, his perspective is limited to cross-sections of the three-dimensional objects that occupy Spaceland. These three dimensional objects appear to him as a fantastic and bewildering array of images, constantly changing shape, appearing and disappearing in thin air.

Flatland: A Romance of Many Dimensions became an instant and enduring success in part because of its biting critique of the bigotry and rigidity of Victorian society (especially its treatment of women) and in part because of its capacity to open its readers' minds to the realms of possibility beyond the experienced senses — even the senses of those of us who experience reality in three dimensions (with time usually considered the fourth). Abbott's work has reminded subsequent generations of readers that our assumptions about reality and our consequent organization of social relations within the reality we perceive may be severely limited. (Even our physical senses are limited: speculation among contemporary scientists includes not merely three, but ten dimensions.)[2] Put in other words, our broken world shapes our capacities of discernment; the world tells us how to perceive reality and how to locate ourselves socially within what we con-

---

2. Michio Kaku, *Hyperspace: A Scientific Odyssey through Parallel Universes, Time Warps, and the 10th Dimension* (New York and Oxford: Oxford University Press, 1994), provides a wonderful, accessible introduction to these matters.

sider reality. In this way our imaginations have become darkened, as Paul puts it (Romans 1:21), and our capacities to discern God's presence in our midst are dulled and diminished.

Easter is the time when Christians should ask hard questions about our dominating perceptions of reality. Does life have to be lived the way we've been taught in the world around us? Must we accept the ways the world constrains us to order our relationships with one another? Are poverty and violence necessarily parts of our human experience? Will there always be strangers and enemies at our doorstep? While much popular theology suggests that we should look for real changes only in "the world to come," the New Testament persistently affirms that God's reality, the realm where Jesus Christ is Lord and Messiah, has already begun to bump into, destabilize and threaten, and finally tear down the most cherished notions of reality our broken world can offer.

Nowhere is this notion of changed reality more clearly and forcefully expressed than in the New Testament's depiction of the resurrected crucified Messiah. The resurrection destroys our notion that death is the final boundary of human experience. The resurrection of Jesus of Nazareth challenges our notion that the powers of this world are the final arbiters of reality. The resurrection of Jesus Christ undermines our notion of a God who is, at best, absent from this world (the premise of secularism) or, at worst, hostile to humankind.

The resurrection is the ultimate vindication of Jesus' way in the world. It is an affirmation that his perception of reality, his organization of relationships, and his way of dealing with the powers of this world is the only true way. The early Christians' proclamation of the Lordship of the resurrected Jesus meant that his story now described for them what it meant to be human. More than even this, the gospel proclamation means that the resurrected Lord now rules both heaven and earth. He is present in power — a power manifested most clearly in the cross — and present to reclaim all of creation for God's glory (cf., e.g., Matthew 28:18-20; Colossians 1:15-20).

But while the New Testament consistently affirms the reality of the resurrection and the continuing presence of Jesus and the Spirit in human experience, the New Testament authors also make it clear that not everyone is able to discern the presence of the resurrected one, save as an anomalous and fleeting apparition. Like Mr. Square observing the fantastic objects in Spaceland, the disciple of Christ catches glimpses here and there of the resurrected Lord, but always just a portion, a *cross*-section, as it were. Moving beyond these experiences — gaining and sustaining sight — requires that disciples nurture a peculiar set of practices and ways of seeing. The disciple must learn to "watch," to "discern," to "see" in such a way that, over time, more and more of the image can be realized. In other words, discerning the presence of the risen Lord requires the nurturing of a peculiar imagination — one shaped by the gospel stories and the practices of discipleship.

The story of the encounter between the risen Jesus and two of his disciples on the road to Emmaus in Luke 24 is one of the richest examples of a large number of gospel stories that are designed to help disciples know where and how to look in order to discern Jesus' presence. The account not only sets forth the essential content of a "resurrection imagination," but also points us toward the settings and practices wherein this peculiar imagination can take shape.

Much like Mr. Square in the story of Flatland, the two disciples on their way to Emmaus are apparently good citizens of their world, hoping only that Jesus would be the one to redeem Israel. They have witnessed his crucifixion at the hands of the chief priests and rulers, those who they understand to hold the ultimate political, economic, and religious power in their world. They understand, according to the world's logic, that Jesus' death means the apparent end of his messianic claims, as well as their own hopes. Thus, they are downcast and standing still when Jesus first encounters them on the road to Emmaus. Passivity and despair are symptoms of imagination and practices held in thrall to the powers of this world. But at least they are on the road, where Jesus always seems to lead his disciples.

He comes among them as a stranger, and uninformed as well. They must tell him all that has taken place in Jerusalem in the last few days. The heart of their account is located in the world's way of imagining things. The bedrock facts of the story are the death of Jesus and the consequent crushing of the disciples' hope. The two disciples can only wonder at the account of the women who were with Jesus at the tomb. The women couldn't find the body, but told of seeing angels who announced that he was alive. Others from the company of disciples went to the tomb, as well, but they did not see him either. This account has all the makings of a scientific breakthrough, a paradigm shift about to happen. All the facts are in, but only some of them count. Those that do not seem to fit the dominant paradigm are cause for wonder and disturbance, but not yet for a new imagination.

Jesus supplies the next required piece. He chides them for being "slow of heart to believe all that the prophets have spoken" (24:25). "Slow of heart" is another way of describing the stupor induced by the world. Jesus addresses this stupor by juxtaposing two things that seem not to belong together in their (and our) imagination. These seemingly paradoxical juxtapositions are one of Jesus' favorite ways of unsettling slow, blind, and faithless disciples. He reminds them that suffering and glory are co-extensive dimensions of the Messiah's way in the world. "Was it not necessary that the Messiah should suffer these things and then enter into his glory?" (24:26). These "bifocal" elements make up the lens through which disciples must learn to look at reality. Moses and the prophets — all of the writings concerning himself — comprise the frame that focuses the disciples' perspective. But still there is no vision. Reports of missing bodies are not enough. Stories of visions are not enough. The Scriptures are not enough. Not even a good sermon, not even one preached by Jesus himself, will penetrate the fog that surrounds these disciples. Discernment of the resurrected Lord requires all these, to be sure. They provide the fragmentary glimpses of what seems to be a fantastic vision. The *cross*-sections of discernment are beginning to pile up, but all these are not yet enough.

Luke locates the turning point of Christian discernment neither in intellectual pursuit nor in words alone, but in the practices of table fellowship with strangers and enemies. As they draw near to the village, Jesus appears to be going on. But they "constrain" him (24:29). The word is surprisingly strong, suggesting coercion, even force. They want him to stay with them. The same Messiah who was born in the stable because there was no place in the inn is now compelled by would-be disciples to remain the night. On their part, this is an act of ideal discipleship. Although his words are already burning in their hearts, he remains a stranger to them. But Jesus has taught and shown them by example that following in his way consists of relentless, surprising acts of hospitality. They have been well-trained, and now, in this most crucial moment, their training pays off. They invite the stranger in.

At table, however, there is another surprise. The stranger be-

34

comes the host. Jesus takes the bread, blesses it, breaks it, and gives it to them. These are eucharistic actions. The disciples have seen Jesus do this before. And now, finally, with these actions their eyes are opened. The text conveys a sense that their recognition is clear, strong, and certain. But as suddenly as Jesus is recognized, he vanishes. We should not seek to resolve the tension this disappearance engenders within us, for it is in these tensions between presence and absence, visibility and invisibility, that the path of discipleship is necessarily located. To dissolve this tension, whether by moving to embrace and control his presence or by resigning ourselves to his absence, is to split open the paradoxical heart of the gospel, the good news of God become human. Resurrection imagination happens in the places where suffering and glory, humanity and divinity, spirit and flesh, presence and absence are embraced.

Those of us in the church are quick to claim the eucharistic setting of discernment toward which this story points, and rightly so. But in our perception of reality, the Eucharist has become a practice that is too often limited to the private confines of the church, where it happens out of sight of the world. We need to remind ourselves that this meal, like the meals Jesus celebrated with the lost ones, the little ones, and the forgotten ones of this world, and like the meals shared by the communities of disciples in early Christianity, was a real meal, not merely a ritualistic symbol. The table of discernment toward which this story points is not the exclusive, homogenous table of most of our churches, but a table with real food shared among strangers.

This risky table is the location not only of discernment but of mission. This story suggests, in fact, that mission and discernment of the risen Lord are co-extensive. Marianne Sawicki has clearly articulated one aspect of the missional dimensions of these verses in her book *Seeing the Lord:* "Luke says that words do not lead anyone to recognize the Risen Lord. In fact, for Luke the ability to recognize a hungry person is the precondition for recognizing the Risen Lord."[3] She situates the Emmaus story within Luke's numerous accounts of hunger and eating in the ministry of Jesus, and concludes that "for Luke . . . recognition of the Risen Lord is possible only within a community that

3. Marianne Sawicki, *Seeing the Lord: Resurrection and Early Christian Practices* (Minneapolis: Fortress Press, 1994), p. 89.

knows both how to be hungry and how to feed the hungry. Stories about empty tombs simply have no efficacy, except within such a community."[4] Discernment of the resurrected Lord does not happen in the solitude of the individual believer's heart, but in the mess and noise of table fellowship with strangers and outcasts.

Luke closes this episode by recording yet another practice of resurrection discernment and imagination. The two disciples rise up from the table that same hour and return to Jerusalem — a place of danger, where the world's powers have crucified Jesus — where they add their story of meeting the resurrected Lord to those already being collected by the rest of the disciples. One of the crucial, yet underdeveloped functions of the worshiping community is to name and gather together the stories of ongoing encounters with the resurrected one. Given the fact that we so infrequently offer contemporary disciples the opportunity and social space to tell their own stories of resurrection encounters, we should not be surprised that resurrection imagination and discernment are so impoverished in many of our churches today. Nurturing a peculiar, Christian vision requires vigilance in naming what we have seen, lest the distorting vision offered by the world suppress our imagination.

Make no mistake about it, entering into the realm of resurrection imagination will entail great personal risk, and the stakes couldn't be higher. When Mr. Square returns from his visit to Spaceland and tries to tell his fellow Flatlanders about the marvels of the third dimension, the High Priests dismiss him as a seditious idiot. His tales of fantastic shapes and images in the third dimension threaten both their tidy belief systems and their organization of the social order. For them, sacredness is located in the meticulous ordering and preservation of a world they can control. At the end of the book, Mr. Square is condemned to spend the rest of his life in solitary confinement, where he cannot threaten their controlled world.

It is not so different for the church. The reordering of power and perception that happens in the cross and resurrection of Jesus Christ has always been a threat to the established powers of this world. For those in the church who are more comfortable with the way things are and with ways of seeing and knowing that are rooted in this world, the

4. Sawicki, *Seeing the Lord*, p. 91.

message of the resurrection will always be an uncomfortable embarrassment, at best. Churches in thrall to the powers of this world will always want to push the resurrection into the next life, into another time or place where it does not encroach upon our tidy, idolatrous ways of perceiving and organizing life.

Luke the evangelist intends the story of the encounter between the risen Jesus and two of his disciples on the road to Emmaus to serve as a challenge precisely to those whose imaginations have become dull and worldly, and whose capacity — or willingness — to discern God's presence has diminished. Luke, like most of the New Testament authors, is not content to let the tomb remain pleasantly empty. Here, rather, we meet a risen Lord who chides us, who challenges us, who makes our hearts burn within us as he accompanies us on the way. But only when we nurture eyes that see and ears that hear.[5]

5. This essay by Stan Saunders originally appeared in the *Journal for Preachers* 20 (Easter 1997): 44-49.

Doughnuts, Coffee, and Communion

In November of 1995 some friends and I (all members of a Sunday School class at Central Presbyterian Church in Atlanta) joined Ed Loring and spent the night with the community of homeless people who stay in the backyard of the Open Door. As our group arrived at 910, the backyard community welcomed us warmly and enthusiastically. Glenda, a homeless woman who served as our host for the night, showed us where to park and gave us each a hug. Already, roles were being reversed; those of us who liked to think of ourselves as providers of hospitality became instead the recipients.

Following dinner with members of the Open Door Community, we ventured out into the cold, each of us carrying three blankets and a piece of cardboard. Glenda and her friends, however, immediately informed us that our supply of cardboard was inadequate; a single piece of cardboard would not provide adequate insulation for a night during which the temperature would dip well down into the thirties. "We'll take you on a cardboard hunt," they announced, and we set out toward the dumpsters on Ponce de Leon.

During the cardboard hunt, the role reversal continued. We middle-class visitors, who were accustomed to being in control, had to give up our privileged positions and take the role of apprentices learning from masters. We were now on the turf of homeless people; they alone knew the essential directions and the unspoken rules. We had no choice but to trust our well-being to this group of strangers. Our trust was not misplaced. Soon we all had enough cardboard to

38

get us through the night, and we returned to 910 and prepared our pallets.

With all of this done, we sat down on the ground in a circle and began to share stories. Those of us who live economically privileged lives were taught about the fragility of life, as our homeless hosts openly told us about their journeys to homelessness. An unfortunate incident, an encounter with the police, an addiction, a divorce — the reasons for homelessness were numerous. However, one thread ran through them all: poor people suffer tremendous consequences for even small mistakes or misfortunes. Incidents that usually have no drastic consequences for middle-class folks — because of our money, our connections, our education, even our self-confidence — can be devastating for those who are poor. How many middle-class folks go to jail for having to urinate? How many wealthy people become homeless because of a divorce or even an addiction, much less because of a traffic violation, which for one of our hosts was the first step toward homelessness? During this intimate time of sharing, the vulnerability of poor people became a tangible reality.

As the evening progressed — from the initial welcome to the cardboard hunt to the shared stories — barriers were slowly being chipped away as roles were reversed. However, the most important event was coming. As the chill began to set in and people began to shuffle around, I noticed that one homeless man — James — had quietly gotten up and left the circle. He went over to a knapsack and rummaged around for a few moments. When he returned, he had a box of doughnuts that he had stashed away to share with the group of visiting strangers. He took the box of doughnuts, broke it open, and gave it to the person next to him, who took a doughnut and passed on the rest. I realized immediately that we were sharing communion. I remembered Jesus — now a black Jesus, a homeless Jesus, an oppressed Jesus — feeding the five thousand with a few loaves and fish. I remembered Jesus sharing meals with outcasts. I remembered Jesus giving bread to his disciples at the Last Supper and at table in Emmaus. James knew we needed to share a meal together. So he brought the doughnuts and gave them to us. And in that odd circle of strangers — rich and poor, black and white, housed and homeless — Jesus was present, and we shared food as equals. It was a joyful, thankful, eucharistic celebration, a foretaste of that great banquet when all God's children will sit together at table in shalom.

The next morning, following a very cold night and a long walk to a labor pool, I witnessed the other half of the communion meal — the cup. As we stood around waiting for Sunday morning breakfast at 910, a conflict arose between Ed Loring and JoJo, a homeless man. JoJo had been trying to break in line to get some coffee, and Ed told him to wait his turn. "I wasn't breaking in line," JoJo responded belligerently, and a confrontation began. As the argument continued, the coffee ran out, leaving none for either Ed or JoJo. JoJo then asked another man standing nearby to share his coffee, which the man did, pouring a generous amount into JoJo's dirty, used cup. With coffee in hand, JoJo became even bolder and defended himself more adamantly: "I would never break in line! I would never try to take something from someone else! I'm always willing to share with others! Man, I'd do anything for anybody who asked me." To which Ed replied, "Okay, then, give me some of your coffee!" JoJo looked quizzically at Ed for a moment. Then he replied, "Sure. Here ya go." And he gave Ed his cup. Ed received the cup, drank a sip of coffee, and then jokingly pretended to gulp down the entire contents. When Ed returned the cup, JoJo burst out laughing, grabbed Ed, and gave him a long, hearty hug. "You're all right, man, you're all right," JoJo laughed.

When Jesus, at the Last Supper, said, "Do this in remembrance of me," he was not simply instituting a sacrament. Jesus was also telling his disciples to continue the table fellowship he had modeled during his time with them — table fellowship with strangers and enemies, tax collectors and sinners, insiders and outsiders. In such table fellowship Jesus is present, breaking down barriers between people and bringing about reconciliation. At such meals our oppressive social order, reinforced in everyday table practices, is undermined, and the reign of God breaks into the world. When we practice Jesus' peculiar "table manners," our activity coincides with God's activity in the world — and that is sacramental.[1] Coffee and doughnuts shared with homeless people embody the kind of communion Jesus desires. "Do *this* in remembrance of me."[2]

1. John Howard Yoder, *Body Politics: Five Practices of the Christian Community Before the Watching World* (Nashville: Discipleship Resources, 1992), pp. 1, 71-73.

2. This essay by Church Camplbell originally appeared in *Hospitality* 15 (June 1996): 1-2.

A Death in the Family[1]

ROMANS 6:1-11; MATTHEW 10:24-39

You've probably heard by now that we are planning to have Carson baptized today, and if you've seen any baptisms lately, especially baptisms of babies, you may be thinking that this will be a pleasant experience, a chance to look at a cute, little baby — the very image of sweetness and purity. You're probably thinking that someone will splash a little water on him, and as a worst case he might cry a bit, and then he will be "saved" — as if by magic — and we can all relax and have a nice supper. If this is your basic sense of things, you're probably not alone, since most of us have witnessed baptisms like this somewhere along the way.

Not long after I moved to Atlanta, I happened to watch a baptism on TV. It was the TV broadcast of a local church service, and the pastor — a kindly looking, older, white-haired man — took this cute little baby in a pretty white gown, said a few words and poured a little water on her head, and then held her up for everyone to see. The people in the church on TV "oooohed" and "aaaahed" and smiled and seemed to think it was all just the nicest thing. Watching this event on TV gave me a kind of critical distance, leading me to the observation that baptism has become, at least in the mainline churches, a benign

---

1. This sermon was preached by Stan Saunders on the occasion of the baptism of Carson Paul Smith-Saunders at the Open Door Community on June 23, 1996; it later appeared in *Hospitality* 15 (September 1996): 6-7.

41

rite, at best a cheap, sugar-coated salvation spectacle, designed mostly to make us feel warm and happy.

When we baptize we are telling a story. And it seems to me that the basic story line most observers would get by watching this ritual in many churches is that pastors are old, babies are cute — even cuter next to old pastors — and that something magical and nice happens when the two of them get together. I do not mean to disparage this image altogether, and I have to admit that I very much enjoy watching babies being baptized, but I do think there is something wrong with this picture. It has to do with what's usually missing. Whatever else we might think is going on during a baptism, there should be no way to avoid the conclusion that while baptism is about new life and celebration, it is also about a death in the family. And I worry that when we baptize without making the reality of this death painfully clear, we are telling a version of the gospel story that has no cross in it. And that just isn't the gospel. So, in case you are tempted to watch what happens here today and merely smile, I need to tell you what will really be going on here.

In a few minutes we are going to put my son Carson to death. And soon after that we hope to raise him again. In fact, if all goes according to plan, these events will happen so quickly that you might think the death didn't really take place. But don't be fooled. Carson Paul Smith-Saunders is going to die today. Brenda and I have come to believe that this is necessary because we no longer trust our capacities, as sinners living in a broken and distorted world, to raise him up in a way that befits the dignity and beauty he possessed at the moment of his birth, and to preserve his life from the powers of violence and death. We are convinced that his ongoing participation in this world will only corrupt and finally destroy him. So, we've decided to give him back to God.

For us, his death today is real, not just a symbol or an abstraction. This reality is tempered only by the hope we hold for what this death means. He will cease to exist under the powers of this world, and will be transformed and transferred to a completely new and different kind of existence, with different powers and possibilities for life, with new eyes to see the world, and most important, with a new family and a new Lord. To use Paul's words, today Carson will be united with Christ in a death like his, he will be buried with him, and he will be crucified with Christ so that the body of sin might be destroyed. And when he is raised up again today, his primary family will no longer be Brenda and myself, or the Smiths and the Saunders, but now it will be all of those who live "in Jesus Christ," especially the family that is the Open Door Community. I want to make very clear what we think this means, first by talking about what Paul and the early Christians meant when they talked about baptism.

In the early chapters of Romans, Paul contrasts the story of Christ with the story of Adam. Adam is the representative character for the typically human story. His story is about disobedience, the fall from grace and the loss of paradise. Adam's life, and the lives of his children, including all of us, is a story of frustration and toil and violence and death. Paul uses the words "sin" and "death" to describe the most important powers in Adam's life, and also in our lives. Because the term "sin" quickly entered the realm of religious language, which usually causes our ears to become heavy and our eyes to glaze over, it needs some fresh unpacking. When Paul talks about sin as a power, he is not thinking, as we usually do, of individual acts that break some law or taboo somewhere. For Paul, sin is the whole fabric of life lived in denial of the reality of a loving and merciful God. Sin is where all of us live, whatever we happen to be doing at the moment — good or bad — when we go about life as if the God of Jesus Christ did not exist.

At the beginning of Romans, Paul suggests that sin is not the cause of our alienation from God, but its symptom. When we choose to turn away from God, and become worshipers of the idols of this world, we inevitably enter a world where sin reigns over us. Sin is thus a powerful stain that covers everything we do and prevents us from seeing clearly and acting rightly. When sin is the dominant reality in our lives, we will necessarily conform our lives to its power — whether by giving in to its patterns and assumptions, for example by practicing the politics of self-interest and domination, or by denying its reality by engaging in pretense and deception. This means that for Paul, sin is not so much about the choices we make to do this or not do that, but about an even more basic loss of freedom and power to make good choices at all. Sin is the loss of freedom and power to become who we were meant to be. And when we have turned away from God and refused to trust God's graciousness, we can no more avoid sin and its consequences than we can avoid breathing in the air. The story of

Adam, then, is the story of life frustrated and held captive by the alien power that Paul calls sin.

We all have our own personal versions of the story of Adam. These versions involve all of the events that have made us who we are — the families we were born into, our losses, our accomplishments in this world. Whatever we bring with us today — our skin color, our gender, our family histories, our stories of abuse and pain, our stories of life on the street, our bad self-esteem, our arrogance and pride, our ambitions and our insecurities — all of these together make up our particular stories in Adam. But the good news Jesus and Paul want to share with us is that we no longer need to live under the power of sin and be defined by our old stories.

According to Paul, there is only one way out of Adam's story of sin and death. We have to learn how to die as Jesus did. Baptism is a training in dying — dying especially to sin and the old self — so that new life can come into being.

Now you might say that Carson doesn't have much of an Adam story yet, but the reality is that his stories of sin and death have been in the planning stage for some time now, just waiting to swing into place at the right moments. The powers of this world have been ready and waiting for Carson to come along, just as they were ready for all of us.

As we all know, in this culture, our humanness is determined by how closely we stand in proximity to the standard that is usually held up as the norm for what it means to be human — white maleness. What do people see when they look at Carson? A boy. A white boy. This determines who he is, how he will be treated, what expectations we have for him, and how he will relate to other people. In real and powerful ways these definitions of humanity and his participation in them will determine what Carson's life means and what his options are.

Today when Carson dies with Christ all of these pieces of his identity, and all of our fleshly hopes and dreams for him, die, too, for baptism means the complete obliteration of this reality and these marks of identity. From this day forward his identity is in Christ, and Christ alone. This is the good news of the gospel. It's precisely what Jesus has in mind when he calls his disciples to give up their lives in order to save them. But, as the mission discourse (Matthew 10) makes clear, there are very real dangers attached to the call to follow Jesus in his mission. Think about how strange Carson's baptism today will make him, and how hard his life will be, after he has been raised from the dead today.

We fully expect that his dying and new life in Christ will eventually make him the butt of jokes and ridicule, like the disciples of Jesus, like Jesus himself, who was called Beelzebub — the King of the garbage pile — by his enemies. We expect that he will find it difficult sometimes to understand and get along with his playmates and peers, who may speak a much different language and have different codes of interaction than he has learned in the community of faith. He will have to struggle throughout most of his life to find ways to shape an identity that is not tied up with his being white and male, and if he succeeds it will make his relationships with women and men and with people of all colors more complex and difficult. He will need to learn to get along with others, and get out of trouble, without turning to domination and intimidation. And we worry that learning these baptismal arts will make him vulnerable. We hope that he will not suffer because he has not learned to use violence to defend himself.

Carson's death today also has important and potentially painful consequences for Brenda and myself. In the first place, we know that if he's going to grow up in the Open Door Community, all of our plans to have him support us in our old age are hopelessly doomed. We also sense that we are not very well equipped to teach him all the things he will need to learn. We know that he will need to work with others of his kind — those who have made the transition from sin and death to life in Christ — to build economic relationships around sharing, gratitude, and dependence on God, rather than exploitation and self-interest; but we know that we are often not very good models or teachers for him in this regard. We know that as a disciple of Jesus he will sometimes have to struggle against his own family, even Brenda and myself, because we have been raised in this world and are too often consumed by the insecurities and addictions of the American middle class. That will cause us pain. Most important, we will have to learn how to love him without possessing him, or seeking to make him in our image, or making him a slave to our own needs, for he will no longer belong to us. We worry about how we can teach him to discern and trust in a God who promises to love and take care of us, when we so often struggle to trust God ourselves. How can we give him up to death, when we fear our own deaths so powerfully?

Of course we wouldn't be here doing this today if it were not for our own baptisms and the hope that God has nourished in us through the years for a new creation. And we wouldn't be *here* today were it not for the hope that we see at work in you all at the Open Door Community. Just as surely as we know that this baptism today marks the death of Carson Paul Smith-Saunders, we also trust that it marks the beginning of a new life, the life of Carson Paul, disciple of the crucified and raised Messiah of Israel and friend of the Open Door Community.

New and different ways of looking at and being in the world can only be sustained in the midst of other people who have also died to this world and whose stories and practices reflect — individually and corporately — their new reality. Carson will receive today a new identity in God, but that new being will only come into its fullness in the midst of a community that also lives in Christ.

I believe that baptism is the doorway into a new social order. Specifically, baptism entails the formation of a new people whose newness and togetherness render all "prior stratifications and classifications" and divisions, all prior stories and social arrangements null and void. Paul talks about this most clearly in Galatians 3, where he says that as many of us as have been baptized into Christ have clothed ourselves with Christ. "There is no longer Jew or Greek, there is no longer slave or free, there is no longer male and female; for all of us are one in Christ Jesus." Now, the unfortunate fact is that it's not very easy to learn this baptismal reality in most churches today.

And that's where the Open Door Community comes into the picture. Today Carson joins the church universal, but he also joins the church particular — in this case the family that is the Open Door Community. We could have had Carson baptized in most any church in the city, but by having him baptized here today, we are intentionally committing him, as well as ourselves, to the peculiar ministry and disciplines of this community. We believe that there are some things he and we can learn only here in the midst of this chaotic, broken, and grace-filled family. And so we are joining our family with yours; and we are entrusting him to you. We hope and trust that you will love him and play with him and share your life with him as fully as you can. But we also have some other things in mind. Specifically, we are trusting you to treat him not as a person of privilege but as another brother and child of God. We hope that you will teach him how to negotiate the

46

streets of the city with compassion, and wisdom, and faith. We want you to help us teach him to respect the dignity of all peoples, including his own God-given dignity, and how to suffer for the sake of others in the name of Jesus Christ. Please, teach him how to stand up and acknowledge the God who is re-creating a fallen world. Teach him how to lend his intelligence, his influence, his hands and voice and body to the mass of humanity that has no hands and no influence. And teach him the arts of mercy and forgiveness and how to hold on to hope in the midst of adversity and suffering.

And while we're teaching him all these things, let's not forget to learn from him — about how to play, how to look at the world through new eyes, and how to give forth perfect praise to God.

There is a death in our family today. Thanks be to God who raises us up every day to live in Christ.

Boys to Men in Atlanta

"Where have I seen his face before?" "That man acts just like somebody I know, but who?" After several Thursday mornings serving at the Butler Street Breakfast, questions like these began to run through my mind. I began to notice men I had seen before, but I couldn't really place them; I had been with them — or someone like them — but I couldn't be sure where. Déjà vu.

I was also having the same experience on Wednesday evenings as I worked with Urban Training Organization of Atlanta at meetings of The Brotherhood, an anti-gang club of African-American boys and young men who live at the Herndon Homes housing project.[1] Located on Northside Drive, Herndon Homes sits in the shadow of the Coca Cola complex and the Georgia Dome, and is just down the street from the new housing for Olympic athletes. During the summer The Brotherhood met in a sweltering-hot community center, which is located in the section of Herndon Homes that has been condemned because of lead poisoning in the ground. ("Don't drink out of the water fountain! You'll get the lead poisoning!" is a regular warning issued to new kids who come to the club.) In this context on Wednesday evenings, I was

1. Urban Training Organization in Atlanta (UTOA) is a community organizing agency that assists urban communities in their efforts toward revitalization and stability and trains theological students, congregations, and others for participation in the urban community. During the time I was volunteering with UTOA, the agency was doing community organizing in several public housing projects in Atlanta.

having the same experience of déjà vu that I was going through in the basement of the Butler Street C.M.E. Church on Thursday mornings.

After wrestling with this experience for several weeks, I finally made the connection. I discovered the link between Herndon Homes and Butler Street. The men's faces that I recognized on Thursday mornings were the faces of young boys with whom I was meeting on Wednesday evenings. The men's faces were older, more tired, and dirtier than those of the boys, but they were recognizable nevertheless. Even some of the personalities were similar. Among the homeless men standing in the grit line or eating their breakfast were adult versions of the young African-American boys with whom I had played the evening before. And on Wednesday evenings, it was the same: at Herndon Homes I found younger, more energetic, less disillusioned embodiments of many of the men I would serve the next morning at Butler Street.

This recurring rhythm — Wednesday evenings in the housing project with young African-American boys and Thursday mornings at Butler Street with homeless African-American men — became a powerful lesson about the way our society deals with poor African-Americans, particularly males. We have two forms of "public housing." Poor African-American women and children are placed in the housing projects. Poor African-American men are "housed" in the shelters and prisons, or else they remain on the streets. And the "powers that be" just seem to be waiting for the young boys in the projects to transfer to the other form of "public housing" when they become adults. For poor African-American males, the movement from boys to men is all too often a predictable movement from one form of public housing to another.

Every Thursday morning I saw the "future" of many of the young boys with whom I had worked on Wednesday evening. And the experience became increasingly painful. After several weeks, I broke down and cried. I had known about racism in my head for a long time (I am, after all, from Little Rock, Arkansas), but, much to my shame, I now cried for the first time — cried over what our society has done and continues to do to a race of people. Moreover, I came to realize that this weeping was the most important theological work I had done in a long time. This weeping was a means of dying — the tears a different form of the waters of baptism. I came to understand that white, middle-class people like myself will begin to live in the new order inaugurated by Jesus Christ only when we have wept — grieved — over our death to the old order in which we enjoy such privilege. For us, such weeping is a way of remembering our baptisms and a necessary precursor to resurrection life.[2]

2. This essay by Chuck Campbell originally appeared in *Hospitality* 15 (May 1996): 2.

The Politics of Worship
in John's Apocalypse[1]

7:9 After this I looked, and there was a great crowd — no one could count all the people! They were from every race, every nation, from every tribe and language, standing before the throne and before the Lamb, dressed in white robes, with palm branches in their hands. 10They cried out in a loud voice, saying, "Salvation belongs to our God, who is seated on the throne, and to the Lamb!" 11And all the angels stood around the throne and around the elders and the four living creatures, and they fell on their faces before the throne and worshiped God, 12singing, "Amen! Blessing and glory and wisdom and thanksgiving and honor and power and might belong to our God forever and ever! Amen." 13Then one of the elders asked me, "Who are these people dressed in white robes, and where have they come from?" 14I said to him, "Sir, you are the one that knows." Then he said to me, "These are the people who have come through the great ordeal; they have washed their robes and made them white in the blood of the Lamb. 15This is why

1. This sermon was preached by Stan Saunders at the Open Door Community on May 3, 1998. It was later published in two parts: "How to Uncover Reality in a World Darkened by the Powers: Reading the Book of Revelation," *Hospitality* 17 (August 1998): 4-5; and "The Witness of Christian Martyrs: The Politics of Worship in John's Apocalypse," *Hospitality* 17 (September 1998): 8-9.

51

they stand before the throne of God, and worship him day and night within his temple. The one who sits on the throne will protect them with his presence. [16]Never again will they hunger or thirst; neither the sun nor the scorching heat will burn them; [17]for the Lamb, who is at the center of the throne, will be their shepherd, and he will guide them to springs of the water of life, and God will wipe away every tear from their eyes."

REVELATION 7:9-17[2]

Within mainstream Christendom over the last two millennia, John's Revelation has been one of the most controversial, least popular, and most misunderstood books. But make no mistake, it is also one of the most important books in the New Testament, especially because of the way it manifests the radical eschatological character of early Christianity. While some have regarded it as an anomaly in the New Testament, Revelation in fact preserves in distinctive form what may have been the "mainstream" perspective of the early Christians as they struggled for survival in the hostile and often violent Empire of Rome.

The most widespread, popular form of religion during the New Testament era was the "cult of the emperors," which held that real power in this world was located in the hands of the Caesars, who were to be worshiped as embodiments of true divinity.[3] In the face of this deeply held cultural perspective, the Christians of the first century believed, preached, and embodied the conviction that the death and resurrection of Jesus Christ was the manifestation of God's true identity and character, the only true and ultimate power in this world. In the imagery of John's Revelation (or "uncovering"), the Lion is not Caesar, but is in fact a Lamb that has been slaughtered! For the author of Revelation, as for the other Christians of the first century, this conviction entailed not merely a change of religious perspectives, but an unmask-

2. Author's translation.
3. See especially Richard A. Horsley, ed., *Paul and Empire: Religion and Power in Roman Imperial Society* (Harrisburg, Pennsylvania: Trinity Press International, 1997).

ing of the false powers of this world and a fundamental reordering of perceptions about time and space.

But we know that the powers of this world remain strong, not least in the churches. For much of the church throughout its history, the logic of the worldly powers has been irresistibly seductive. And John's Revelation has itself been one of the chief victims of this turn in the churches toward the power and rationality of fallen creation. Among many Christians today this book has been reduced to an esoteric code describing the events and persons associated with "the end of the world," or a cryptic timetable for doomsday scenarios of violent revenge. Among these people, John's vision of the slaughtered Lamb may be at best a side point. And the present-time focus of John's vision, which affirms the present as a time of grace, resistance, and new creation, is likely to be overshadowed. On the other hand, many other circles in the North American church today virtually refuse to read Revelation. They regard it as an embarrassing problem, more the cause of frustration and confusion than a source of true vision and hope. In either case, John's voice is muffled and the visionary quality of the book is blurred — and the powers of this world continue their domination of our experience and imagination.

The problem, as we can begin to see, lies not so much with the character of Revelation itself as with the character of the churches. Unless one reads from the perspective of the poor and the oppressed — and especially from the perspective of the Christian martyrs — this book will remain hopelessly confusing at best, and will probably even be an affront. To those in established, comfortable churches, John's Revelation addresses a critical voice (chs. 2-3). It presses without compromise for radical reform of the church and more faithful ways of being Christian.

Throughout the history of the church, Christian readers in situations of oppression and injustice have found in Revelation not only visions of hope for the future, but a voice of resistance — especially to authoritarian and exclusive expressions of power. Revelation resists even quiet complicity with any power that is used to deny the dignity and steal the life of the poor. That is why this book is so important for those who work for the cause of Christ among poor and homeless people today. For these witnesses, Revelation can be a source of powerful encouragement and discernment. But where those who profess the name of Christ turn a blind eye to the poor, where they say that the homeless have only themselves to blame, you can bet that the message of Revelation has not been heard lately. As the Latin American theologian Pablo Richard so astutely notes, "It was disregard of Revelation that opened the way for the incorporation of the Church into the dominant imperial system and the construction of an authoritarian Christendom. To retrieve Revelation is to retrieve a fundamental dimension of the Jesus movement and of the origins of Christianity."[4]

Given the socially and culturally rooted distortions that most of us bring to our reading of Revelation, some reorientation of our assumptions and reading strategies is in order. First, *what* is John's Revelation essentially about? At the most basic level, John wants to tell us that things are not what they seem. John's Revelation is about the discrepancy between appearances and reality, especially as this pertains to the apparent dominance of the powers of this world. The Lamb reigns, and because of this everything is being made new. While Revelation has been read as predictions about the future, or about the end of history, its perspective is more basically oriented toward the present — and especially to the experience of those who are aware of the discrepancies between appearances and reality. This last aspect is one of the elements that make this book important especially for poor and homeless people, for they are often more in touch with the discrepancies between appearances and reality than those of us who, owing to our wealth, participate more fully in the visions of reality mediated to us by the larger culture.

Then *what does John tell us about the end of the world?* John's Revelation unmasks (i.e., reveals, uncovers) the frailty of the powers and structures that fallen humankind regards as absolute. In this way Revelation helps us discern those forces that are driving creation to the brink of crisis. We learn from Revelation that what the citizens of the Roman Empire have been told are the forces of salvation and justice are, in fact, the forces of death. But we also learn that because of the rule of the Lamb, the apparent victory of these forces is only illusory. In other words, Revelation tells us that the end of the world is not only

---

4. Pablo Richard, *Apocalypse: A People's Commentary on the Book of Revelation* (Maryknoll, New York: Orbis Books, 1995), p. 3. My indebtedness to Richard's work looms large throughout this sermon.

about to happen, but that it already *is* happening and *has been* accomplished in our midst — in the life, death, and resurrection of a Galilean Jew nearly two thousand years ago.

Then *why should we bother to read it today?* John's Apocalypse has been most important in times of social chaos — persecution, exclusion, and ongoing oppression. John's visions nurture a spirituality of resistance and provide the imaginative resources and courage for organizing an alternative world. In a world where market mentalities prevail, where people are turned into commodities, where capitalism and materialism claim victory in the name of freedom and democracy, and where poverty and homelessness are criminalized, Christians can no longer afford to ignore and distort John's message. And especially for those who struggle for justice against apparently insurmountable forces, this book is must reading.

How, then, do we make sense of this strange book? Our reading strategies when we come to this book should be focused primarily on the character of our communities and our relational priorities. The great mistake of most Christians has been in thinking that no one, except perhaps the professional interpreters, can make sense of this book. The great mistake of many professional interpreters has been in presuming that anyone with the right skills or the right code could make sense of this book. But that has never really been the case. Revelation is addressed to and best understood by the poor, the oppressed, the outcast. The rich and powerful probably cannot or will not make sense of John's Apocalypse. If we want to make sense of this book, but we are most closely allied with the rich and powerful, we need to exert every effort to close the gap between ourselves and the poor and oppressed who live in our front yard. In other words, in order to make sense of Revelation, we need to be less concerned about its esoteric symbols and more concerned about who we are standing with and whose voices we are listening to.

This means that we need to learn to read this book within the context of the worshiping community of martyrs. But in order to align our vision with John's, we may need to consider two of these terms — worship and martyrs — in fresh ways. Throughout this book, which is filled with the language and imagery of worship, worship is not merely what "churchy" people do in the safe void of sanctuaries, but rather a form of sanctuary that is discerned in the presence of the crucified Christ. Throughout Revelation worship is particularly what the martyrs are found doing. The English term *martyr* is related to the Greek word for testimony — martyrs are those who testify with their lives. In Revelation, the martyrs' expressions of worship look at times suspiciously like what we might call political action, for their worship involves unmasking the empty claims of the powers by witnessing to the Lamb. Their witness includes proclamation of truth in the face of oppression and injustice, often involving events — such as the crucifixion of the Galilean peasant, the judgment of oppressors, and the protection of the holy ones — of which the ordinary inhabitants of the Roman Empire would scarcely be aware. But in every case, the martyrs are present, putting their bodies on the line in a form of worship that cannot be hidden and that the world cannot deny.

For John, the heavenly realities to which the martyrs witness do not exist somewhere else beyond this world, but are continually present within Christian experience (though usually hidden at least to the world). The worship of those who testify on behalf of the Lamb is the space and time where the earthly and heavenly realms touch. The faithful worship of Revelation happens not so much in the private experience of the congregations described in chapters 2 and 3, but in those spaces where the witness of the martyrs publicly confronts the powers of empire. In this way, the truths to which Revelation points are inextricably embedded in history, rather than in escape from history. The worship John describes taking place both in heaven and on earth thus participates in God's liberation of creation from oppression and death for the sake of a new creation in which God's glory becomes visible over the whole world.

John's Revelation, in short, is the revelation of God's presence in this world for the sake of the people we see every day in the yard of the Open Door Community — the poor, the outcast, and the oppressed. What seems to be true, John reveals, is not true in reality. The powers of this world will not stand, but only the crucified Lamb. Revelation calls the church to public, embodied worship, testifying to the power of the Lamb that was slain. While much of contemporary Christendom may find these images obscure or objectionable, those who continue to seek the face of Jesus among poor and homeless people cannot afford to pursue their calling without the vision, the honesty, and the hope of John's Revelation.

The only appropriate setting for our perception of the realities John describes, as well as for a more accurate discernment of the message of Revelation itself, is the worshiping community of the oppressed — the martyrs who offer their very lives as testimony to the reign of the Lamb. We can see this clearly in Revelation 7:9-17. As is true of much of Revelation, the setting of these verses is worship. We know this first of all by the identification of the primary actors described in these verses. Who are these here gathered before the throne of God? John describes them as those who have come through the great ordeal and have washed their robes in the blood of the Lamb. Not merely the nice people, not merely those in clean suits and pretty hats. And certainly not respectable folks in the eyes of the world. Those who have come through the ordeal — the tribulation — are earlier described as those who bear the seal or mark of the Lamb written on their foreheads. The mark of the Lamb designates not just a physical mark, but a belonging; the mark is put upon those who follow a way of life and pursue practices that defy the idols of this world. The mark is upon those who have resisted the powers of this world to the point of death. They are the martyrs, those who witness at the cost of their lives to the power of a crucified Messiah. They come from every race, nation, tribe, and language, defying the conventional divisions of the world. The ordeal they have come through is the persistent suffering, oppression, imprisonment, exclusion, violence, rejection, and finally death by which the system resists their worship of Jesus Christ. Theirs is not worship for the sake of impressions, but worship in the face of death. They now wear purified clothing, robes that have been soaked in the Lamb's blood.

It is crucial for us to recognize the political character of this worship in the words spoken by the martyrs. The worship language that John cites in these verses may sound rather ordinary to us, but for John and the rest of the first-century church, this language was the cultic and political language of the Roman Empire. The political rhetoric of the day claimed that salvation and peace were the gift — the grace — of the Caesars, that faith was a matter of putting one's trust in the emperor. Justice and righteousness consisted in being a good citizen of the empire, abiding by all its laws, and finding one's right place, whether as free or slave, within the existing social structures. This language wasn't borrowed by the empire from the Christians, but by the

Christians from the empire. What we have come to know as religious language of the Christian faith was in fact the political language of the reigning powers of the empire. Christians like John took the words being spoken about Caesar and the empire and related them instead to Jesus.

These Christians believed real power lay not in the hands of the emperors — the rich, the powerful, or the military leaders — but with the Lamb who was slain. In other words, where the world wants to turn words like peace, freedom, justice, faith, and grace into empty platitudes, John wants to use these terms to describe another reality, the rule of the Lamb. The cry of those gathered around the throne of God in verse 10 — "Salvation belongs to our God, who is seated on the throne, and to the Lamb" — is not church talk, but a social and political claim about the real ruler of the world. "Blessing and glory and wisdom and thanksgiving and honor and power and might belong to our God forever and ever" (v. 12) is not empty doxology, but powerful and provocative praise in the face of the contrary claims of the Roman Empire.

The opening of the sixth seal, of which these verses are the culmination, describes reality not only in the first-century context of John's community, but also in the present, wherever and whenever the poor and the oppressed — the people we know on the streets of Atlanta — endure the chaos of life in the hands of empire. We ought to remember this message particularly where the world offers competing visions of reality. Does Bill Gates have the operating system of the future? No, the Lamb who was slain does. Does Central Atlanta Progress know how to make a beautiful city? No, the Lamb who was slain does. Does the criminal justice system know how to make our streets safe again? No, only the Lamb who was slain. Can we trust the insurance companies to provide a secure future for our families? No, only the Lamb who was slain. Is Coca-Cola really the real thing? No, only the Lamb who was slain. Blessing and glory and wisdom and honor and power and might belong not to the powers of this world, but to our God!

In the end, Revelation is not only an account of John's visions and convictions, but more particularly a book of prayer. We are living today in a time of crisis, not unlike the time when John experienced his visions of heaven and earth in ultimate crisis. We ought to be concerned about what lies before us, just as the first readers of this book were. We are witnessing unprecedented ecological, political, social, and economic crises. Meanwhile the powers are telling us that the economy is getting stronger, that global warming cannot be proven, that our lives are better than ever before, and that the poor are that way because they choose to be. Revelation warns us that things are getting worse, and the worst is yet to come. It warns us that those who are already poor and oppressed will bear the brunt of the suffering to come. We have every right to be afraid.

But it also assures us that God is working to reclaim what has been broken. Despite all appearances, the Lamb who was slain now rules. This is not a conviction that should lead us to passivity, but rather a vision that calls us to continue to witness faithfully to the one who sits on the throne. And so I invite us to pray together with John today that our witness may be with words that are true and with bodies that are strong to endure whatever suffering the world puts before us for the sake of the Lamb. Let our hope be set on the day when

> The one who sits on the throne will protect us with his presence. Never again will we hunger or thirst; neither the sun nor the scorching heat will burn us; for the Lamb, who is at the center of the throne, will be our shepherd, and he will guide us to springs of the water of life, and God will wipe away every tear from our eyes. (7:15-17)

And let the prayer we give expression to, both with our words and our bodies, be the prayer of the martyrs: "Salvation belongs to our God, who is seated on the throne, and to the Lamb."

WORD

And the Word became flesh and lived among us. . . .

Total Immersion

Etching with aquatint; 16" × 12"; © 1996 Christina Bray

The Streets, the Powers, and the Word: Learning from William Stringfellow

In the face of death, live humanly. In the middle of chaos, celebrate the Word. Amidst babel . . . speak the truth. Confront the noise and verbiage and falsehood of death with the truth and potency and efficacy of the Word of God. Know the Word, teach the Word, nurture the Word, preach the Word, defend the Word, incarnate the Word, do the Word, live the Word. And more than that, in the Word of God, expose death and all death's works and wiles, rebuke lies, cast out demons, exorcise, cleanse the possessed, raise those who are dead in mind and conscience.

WILLIAM STRINGFELLOW, *An Ethic for Christians
and Other Aliens in a Strange Land*, p. 143

Several years ago I was having lunch at a soup kitchen that serves homeless people in Atlanta. As I was eating, a man at my table looked at me with a touch of madness in his eyes and commented, "You know, the Devil is alive!" Taken completely off guard by his comment, I muttered something like, "Oh, really? How do you know?" The man stared at me for a moment as if I were the one who was crazy. Then he replied, "Just look around!" As I gazed around the room filled with homeless, hungry African-American men, I began to understand. That room could not be explained in terms of individual sins or failings, though many in our individualistic culture still naively presume such an interpretation. Rather, these were men whose lives were subject to powers over which they had no control. Something larger and more ominous than mere human will, something of enormous and disturbing power, something that smelled of death — something indeed demonic — was at work. The homeless man spoke to me like Jesus: "Do you have eyes, and fail to see?" (Mark 8:18). And he introduced me to what the New Testament calls the "principalities and powers."

William Stringfellow on the Principalities and Powers[1]

It was in a similar physical and social location that William Stringfellow, the Harvard-educated lawyer, lay theologian, and radical Christian, developed his groundbreaking understanding of the principalities and powers.[2] Following his graduation from Harvard Law School, Stringfellow moved to East Harlem, where he lived and practiced street law for seven years.[3] Immersing himself in the Bible while listening to the people of East Harlem, Stringfellow began to develop his theology of the powers.[4] In Harlem, Stringfellow

> attended at once to the Word and to the people. And he credited the latter with pointing him to the former. For example, the people on

1. For a helpful overview of Stringfellow's work on the principalities and powers, see Bill Wylie Kellermann, ed., *A Keeper of the Word: Selected Writings of William Stringfellow* (Grand Rapids: Eerdmans, 1994), pp. 185-292. This book offers the best single introduction to Stringfellow's life and thought.

2. Stringfellow's work inspired and informed the well-known trilogy on the powers by Walter Wink: *Naming the Powers* (Philadelphia: Fortress Press, 1984); *Unmasking the Powers* (Philadelphia: Fortress Press, 1986); *Engaging the Powers* (Philadelphia: Fortress Press, 1992).

3. Stringfellow wrote about his years in East Harlem in his book *My People Is the Enemy: An Autobiographical Polemic* (New York: Holt, Rinehart, and Winston, 1964).

4. Andrew W. McThenia, Jr., "Introduction: How This Celebration Began," in *Radical Christian and Exemplary Lawyer*, ed. Andrew W. McThenia, Jr. (Grand Rapids: Eerdmans, 1995), p. 8.

the street first clued him in on the biblical import of the principalities. He would hear folks speak of the gas company, the slum real estate lords, the social bureaucracies, the city administration, the Mafia, and police agencies as though they were predatory beasts, arrayed against the neighborhood and human beings, eating them alive. His writings have since become notorious, among other things for explicating a biblical doctrine of the powers as precisely that: fallen and predatory creatures, acting with an independent life of their own.[5]

Although in his early book, *Free in Obedience*, Stringfellow defined these predatory creatures as ideologies, institutions, and images, his understanding of the principalities was in fact very broad and rather unsystematic, as became evident in his later writing.[6] In *An Ethic for Christians and Other Aliens in a Strange Land*, his most important treatment of the powers, Stringfellow emphasized that the powers are legion:

> The very array of names and titles in biblical usage for the principalities and powers is some indication of the scope and significance of the subject for human beings. And if some of these seem quaint, transposed into contemporary language they lose quaintness and the principalities become recognizable and all too familiar: they include all institutions, all ideologies, all images, all movements, all causes, all corporations, all bureaucracies, all traditions, all methods and routines, all conglomerates, all races, all nations, all idols.[7]

The powers, in short, are many-faceted and versatile; they are "potent and mobile and diverse, not static or neat. . . ."[8] As Walter Wink has

---

5. Bill Wylie Kellermann, "Bill, the Bible, and the Seminary Underground," in McThenia, ed., *Radical Christian and Exemplary Lawyer*, p. 68.

6. On the principalities as ideologies, institutions, and images, see William Stringfellow, *Free in Obedience* (New York: Seabury Press, 1964), pp. 52-59.

7. William Stringfellow, *An Ethic for Christians and Other Aliens in a Strange Land* (Waco, Texas: Word Books, 1973; 3rd paperback ed., 1979), p. 78.

8. Stringfellow, *An Ethic for Christians*, p. 79. According to Stringfellow, the preeminent principality is the state. See *An Ethic for Christians*, pp. 107-11.

written, "the powers comprise all of social, political, and corporate reality, in both visible and invisible manifestations."[9]

Although these principalities and powers are creatures of God, with the vocation of sustaining life in society, they are fallen; they exist in a moral state of death, which characterizes the fall. Claiming autonomy from God and dominion over human beings and the rest of creation, the principalities and powers have forgotten their creatureliness and repudiated their vocation. They have become relentlessly aggressive against all of life, particularly human life in society.

Assuming the place of God in the world, the powers want to dominate human beings and seek to crush any resistance to their dominion.[10] Death — physical, political, social, personal, and especially moral — is their ultimate power and sanction.[11] The principalities and powers ultimately become demonic, having such dehumanizing purposes that they must be said to be governed by the power of death.[12] For the powers, finally, the only morality that matters is their own survival. "The principalities have great resilience; the death game which they play continues, adapting its means of dominating human beings to the sole morality which governs all demonic powers so long as they exist — survival."[13] In relation to these aggressive principalities, human beings have the status of captives and victims, whether we serve gladly as acolytes to the powers or simply acquiesce to our captivity in silence and complacency.[14]

9. Walter Wink, "Stringfellow on the Powers," in McThenia, ed., *Radical Christian and Exemplary Lawyer*, p. 26. For Wink's more systematic definition of the powers, see *Naming*, p. 5.

10 Stringfellow, *An Ethic for Christians*, p. 51.

11. Stringfellow, *An Ethic for Christians*, p. 81. Stringfellow uses "death" in the broadest possible sense: "Thus, in this book, when the name of death is used, I intend that it bear *every* definition and nuance, *every* association and suggestion, *every* implication and intuition that *anyone* has *ever* attributed to death, and I intend that the name of death, here, bear all meanings simultaneously and cumulatively" (*An Ethic for Christians*, p. 69).

12. Stringfellow, *An Ethic for Christians*, p. 32. "Demonic," for Stringfellow, does not simply mean "evil." Rather, the "demonic" involves death and fallenness; it is a state of separation from life, bondage to death, and alienation from God. See Stringfellow, *Free in Obedience*, pp. 62-64.

13. Stringfellow, *An Ethic for Christians*, p. 93.

14. Stringfellow, *An Ethic for Christians*, pp. 86-89.

In order to retain this control over human beings and insure their own survival, the powers use a variety of tactics or stratagems, many of them verbal. Indeed, according to Stringfellow, the verbal is "definitive in all the ploys of the principalities"; babel becomes the prevailing form of existence — a fact that should be of particular interest to those of us who seek to discern, live, and proclaim the Word.[15]

> Babel means the inversion of language, verbal inflation, libel, rumor, euphemism and coded phrases, rhetorical wantonness, redundancy, hyperbole, such profusion in speech and sound that comprehension is impaired, nonsense, sophistry, jargon, noise, incoherence, a chaos of voices and tongues, falsehood, blasphemy.[16]

In the place of truthful speech, we encounter the propaganda of the state, the exaggerations of Madison Avenue, the doublespeak of politicians, the false claims of expertise by bureaucrats, the code language of racism, the silent secrecy of corporations, and the diversions of entertainment.[17] The result of these and other tactics is the demoralization of human beings — literally, the death of the moral conscience. As Stringfellow writes,

> The relentlessness of multifarious babel in America, for example, has wrought a fatigue both visceral and intellectual in millions upon millions of Americans. By now truly *de*moralized, they suffer no conscience and they risk no action. Their human interest in living is narrowed to meager subsisting; their hope for life is no more than avoiding involvement with other humans and a desire that no one will bother them. They have lost any expectations for society; they have no stamina left for confronting the principalities; they are reduced to docility, lassitude, torpor, profound apathy, and default. The demoralization of human beings in this fashion greatly conveniences the totalitarianism of the demonic powers since the need to

---

15. Stringfellow, *An Ethic for Christians,* p. 98.

16. Stringfellow, *An Ethic for Christians,* p. 106.

17. For Stringfellow's detailed discussion of the verbal ploys of the powers, see *An Ethic for Christians,* pp. 98-106.

resort to persecutions or imprisonment is obviated, as the people are already morally captive.[18]

Although violence and war remain the ultimate sanctions of the powers, babel can also produce the moral death that is the province of the principalities and powers.

For Christians, however, the reality of death embodied in the powers is not the final Word. Rather, Christians also know the reality and power of the resurrection, which enables believers to live now in resistance to the power of death in the world. In his life, death, and resurrection, Jesus engaged the powers and won victory over them. Participating in Christ's victory, Christians can similarly resist the powers.[19] Despite Stringfellow's stark portrayal of a fallen world in the grip of the powers of death, he remains a theologian of hope. "The good news to the world is that we can stop living in thrall to the powers now, even under the conditions of death. The gospel is that God sets us free from the dread of death, the cajolery of death, and the seductiveness of death, even though we are complicit with death's power."[20] In the power of the resurrection, we can, in Stringfellow's terms, begin to live humanly in the face of death.[21]

The living Word of God, Stringfellow affirms, is present and active in every moment, even in the midst of death. "So, in the same event, in any happening whatever, there is the moral reality of death and there is the incarnation of the Word of God, the demonic and dehumanizing and the power of the Resurrection, the portents of the Apocalypse impending and the signs of the imminence of the Escha-

18. Stringfellow, *An Ethic for Christians,* p. 106.

19. Stringfellow draws upon a Christus Victor understanding of Jesus' work. See Gustaf Aulen, *Christus Victor* (New York: Macmillan, 1931). For contemporary treatments of the Christus Victor model of the atonement see J. Denny Weaver, "Atonement for the Nonconstantinian Church," *Modern Theology* 6 (July 1990): 307-23; and Gayle Gerber Koontz, "The Liberation of Atonement," *Mennonite Quarterly Review* 63 (April 1989): 171-92.

20. Wink, "Stringfellow," p. 20.

21. The character of "living humanly" cannot be reduced to general principles or universal rules. Nor can it be simplistically equated with "doing the will of God." Living humanly is, rather, a very human venture characterized by freedom from the bondage of death and involving response to the incarnate Word in specific circumstances.

ton."[22] For Christians the fundamental ethical challenge and possibility becomes discerning the incarnate, living Word of God amidst the realities of death and, in response to the Word, living free from the bondage of death. Such "resistance to death is the only way to live humanly in the midst of the fall."[23]

Because for Stringfellow there is no such thing as an individualistic Christianity, the church plays an essential role in this resistance.[24] In the midst of death, the church's vocation in and for the world is to witness to the Word and be a community of resistance. The church is called to be a community of "resident aliens, separate from the world so it can tell the truth to . . . the principalities and powers."[25] The eschatological gifts of the Spirit — discernment, glossolalia, healing, and exorcism, all politically interpreted — empower the church's discernment, resistance, and hope: "These gifts dispel idolatry and free human beings to celebrate Creation, which is, biblically speaking, integral to the worship of God. The gifts equip persons to live humanly in the midst of the Fall. The exercise of these gifts constitutes the essential tactics of resistance to the power of death."[26]

The church itself, however, exists in the tension between bondage to death and freedom in the Word. On the one hand, Stringfellow had stinging criticisms for the institutional church in America. The church not only often serves the powers of the world, particularly the nation, but even functions as one of the powers itself.[27] The church is far too often obsessed with its own survival and "engaged in the elaborate worship of death."[28] The only hope seems to lie in a "confessing movement" scattered here and there, now and then in some congregations, paracongregations, and intentional communities.[29]

---

22. Stringfellow, *An Ethic for Christians*, p. 152.

23. Stringfellow, *An Ethic for Christians*, p. 138.

24. Stringfellow, *An Ethic for Christians*, p. 61.

25. McThenia, "Introduction," p. 10.

26. Stringfellow, *An Ethic for Christians*, p. 145; emphasis omitted. For Stringfellow's extended discussion of the gifts of the Spirit, see pp. 138-51.

27. Stringfellow, *Free in Obedience*, pp. 77-89; *An Ethic for Christians*, pp. 57-59, 121; see also William Stringfellow, *A Private and Public Faith* (Grand Rapids: Eerdmans, 1962).

28. Stringfellow, *An Ethic for Christians*, p. 58.

29. Stringfellow, *An Ethic for Christians*, pp. 59-61, 122.

On the other hand, Stringfellow had a grand vision of what the church is by the Word of God and the gift of the Spirit. The church, he could write, is the "foretaste and forerunner . . . of the reconciled society"; it is "the image of God's own Kingdom, of the Eschaton."[30] The church, particularly as it gathers in its eucharistic worship, is an embodiment of the beloved community.

> In seeing the gathered congregation the world has a glimpse of the Kingdom of Christ. This is the only apparent image of the community reconciled with God in which the members are also reconciled to themselves, to each other, to all [people], and to all of creation. The worshiping congregation is the only evidence of the Christian society's existence in the world, and it is the exemplification of that which the world is called to be and of that which is vouchsafed by the ministry of Christ.[31]

Called to be the "holy nation" that resists the powers and embodies an alternative, the church itself lives in the tension between its bondage to death and its freedom in the Spirit.

Stringfellow thus argues that the principalities and powers provide the fundamental ethical context for the Christian life, which is characterized by resistance and hope. Karl Barth's words about Stringfellow, spoken at a panel discussion during Barth's visit to the United States in 1962, should be heeded by contemporary Christians: "You should listen to this man!"[32]

Practices of Resistance and Hope

Stringfellow not only developed a theology of the powers. He also embodied a life of resistance and hope. In his eulogy for Stringfellow, Daniel Berrigan praised him as a "keeper of the Word," a comment

30. Stringfellow, *Free in Obedience*, p. 103.
31. Stringfellow, *Free in Obedience*, p. 43. Because Stringfellow himself moved toward the use of inclusive language in his later work, I have taken the liberty of substituting inclusive language in some quotations.
32. Kellermann, *Keeper of the Word*, p. 1.

that captures well Stringfellow's faithful discipleship.[33] Another writer has referred to Stringfellow as "a parable before the powers."[34] Indeed, in a distinctive way Stringfellow's theology emerged from the peculiar practices that shaped his life.

Stringfellow's life thus suggests the importance of particular practices of resistance and hope in confrontation with the principalities and powers. One practice was central to all the others: reading Scripture in the context of the streets. It is not surprising that Stringfellow developed his theology of the powers as he listened to the poor, the most visible victims of the powers, while immersing himself in the Bible, which exposes the powers and offers an alternative vision. It was the conjunction of physical/social location and Bible study that opened Stringfellow's eyes to the predatory character of the principalities. Here Stringfellow offers a challenge to all mainstream, middle-class Christians.[35]

Although few of us will actually move to a place like East Harlem, even small attempts to be with and listen to poor people entail active resistance to the powers within the context of contemporary middle-class life. Indeed, the very effort to spend significant time among those who are poor immediately confronts Christians with the realities of the powers, including the institutional church, which are actively at work in the world to keep middle-class people and poor people apart. If these two groups were to spend much time together, the fallout for the churches might be enormous — and threatening. Moreover, the ploys of the powers are subtle and deceptive at this point. Of these ploys, one is particularly prominent today: busyness.

Busyness has become a characteristic of middle-class life, including the lives of pastors. Almost everywhere I go I hear complaints about how busy people are — and I echo those complaints myself almost daily. Amidst the constant demands of daily life, many of us cannot imagine spending significant time among poor people — not doing *for* them (to justify our time?), but listening to them and learning from them. We just don't have the time. Normally, however, we treat

33. Kellermann, *Keeper of the Word*, p. xii.

34. Bill Wylie Kellermann, "Listen to This Man: A Parable Before the Powers," *Theology Today* 53 (October 1996): 301.

35. In *Free in Obedience,* Stringfellow directly issues such a challenge to church leaders. See pp. 40-42.

this busyness as simply a rather unfortunate characteristic of life — and ministry — today.

Stringfellow's work, however, reminds us that "diversion" is one of the stratagems the powers employ to maintain their power. When seen from this perspective, busyness takes on a more insidious appearance. It is one way the principalities divert us from seeing and responding to the realities of death in the world. It is one of the ways the powers *de*moralize human beings. When middle-class folks, including pastors, become too busy to notice or care about anything beyond their daily routines, the powers have diverted one more potential challenge to their dominion in the world. As one woman recently commented to me, "By the end of the day, when I can finally sit down at home, I'm too tired to care about anything else going on in the world." Such busyness is not simply an unfortunate aspect of contemporary life. It is rather one way middle-class folks are held captive by the powers.[36]

One of the most important acts of resistance in which Christians can engage involves taking the time — literally taking it back from the powers — to become apprentices to those who are poor, homeless, imprisoned, or abused. Such a commitment not only announces a clear "No!" to the powers who would kill our moral conscience, but also provides the essential context for discerning and resisting the principalities and powers. For, as Stringfellow reminds us, it is among those who are poor and oppressed that we see most graphically the aggressive, predatory character of the powers.

Simply being "on the streets," however, was not adequate for Stringfellow. The streets, rather, provided the necessary context for reading the Bible and discerning God's Word in the world. In conjunction with the voices of those on the margins, recourse to the Bible was for Stringfellow "a primary, practical, and essential tactic of resistance."[37] From this practice too the powers will desperately seek to divert us, for the Bible not only names and exposes the principalities that hold people captive, but also provides the memories of God's faithfulness and the promise of Jesus' resurrection, which give believers hope. Indeed, faithful confrontation with the powers of death requires con-

---

36. See Stringfellow, *An Ethic for Christians*, pp. 90-91.
37. Stringfellow, *An Ethic for Christians*, p. 120; italics omitted.

stant immersion in the "world of the Bible," as Stringfellow himself noted in his book *Instead of Death:*

> I spend most of my life now with the Bible, reading or more precisely listening. My mundane involvements . . . have become more and more intertwined with this major preoccupation of mine, so that I can no longer readily separate one from the others.
>
> This merging for me of almost everything into a biblical scheme of living occurs because the data of the Bible and one's existence in common history is characteristically similar. One comes, after a while, to live in a continuing biblical context and so is spared both an artificial compartmentalization of one's person and a false pietism in living.[38]

Such an immersion in Scripture empowers us for lives of resistance and hope.

This biblically shaped way of life requires community, for no individual is a match for the ploys and pressures and sanctions of the powers. Indeed, Jesus himself enacted this resistance and hope primarily in his practice of table fellowship with "sinners," who consisted largely of poor people unable to follow all the legal regulations of the day. And, not surprisingly, the hospitality of table fellowship became an important aspect of Stringfellow's later life, as his home on Block Island, Rhode Island, became a place of hospitality for many and diverse people. In small, alternative communities gathered around Scripture and the eucharistic table of Jesus, resistance and hope are nurtured and sustained in the face of the power of death.

Such communities may even be necessary to help pastors resist the pressures of the institutional church itself. As an institution, the church, like all the powers, is obsessed with its own survival and prefers "safe" pastors who will not threaten its comfortable existence. Whether subtly or directly, the institutional church will press pastors to accommodate themselves to the status quo. Despite their best intentions and ideals, pastors easily become servants of the in-

---

38. William Stringfellow, *Instead of Death* (New York: Seabury, 1976), pp. 3-4. Quoted in Kellermann, "Seminary Underground," p. 56. See also Stringfellow, *An Ethic for Christians*, p. 120.

stitution, driven by its demands and aspiring to its standards of success. Salary, buildings, membership, titles, perks, popularity, and influence become the focus — not unlike the standards of "success" in other institutions. Slowly, almost imperceptibly, the powers wear pastors down and make them numb; the rough edges of the gospel are worn away.

In this context, pastors, like all other Christians who would dare to confront the principalities and powers, will need to find or create small communities that will nurture them, sustain them, and hold them accountable.[39] Rooted in such alternative communities, pastors may be built up in the practices of resistance and hope. And the church's ministry may indeed become the faithful expression of disciples who are "keepers of the Word."

Preaching as Resistance

In the midst of death, in the face of the powers, in the power of the Word, Christians take a stance of resistance — often "audacious, extemporaneous, fragile, puny, foolish" resistance.[40] One form of this resistance, as has been said, involves reading Scripture "on the streets" in community. Another form of this resistance is preaching.[41] Moreover, because of the verbal nature of the powers' tactics, preaching, as the counterspeech of the Word of God, can be a particularly important form of resistance. As Stringfellow encourages, "Amidst babel, I re-

39. On small communities of resistance, see Stringfellow, *An Ethic for Christians*, pp. 121-22.

40. Stringfellow, *An Ethic for Christians*, p. 119.

41. On preaching as a practice of nonviolent resistance, see Charles L. Campbell, "Performing the Scriptures: Preaching and Jesus' Third Way," *Journal for Preachers* 17 (Lent 1994): 18-24. Although Stringfellow recognizes the violent character of the powers, including the violence of babel, he does not stress nonviolent resistance as consistently as Walter Wink. Stringfellow's concern for the freedom of God and his understanding of the powers made him suspicious of all ideologies, including "ideological pacifism." Recently, however, Wink has persuasively argued that the logic of Stringfellow's work leads to nonviolence. On this particular issue, I find Wink's position most compelling. See Stringfellow, *An Ethic for Christians*, pp. 106-7, 122-33; Wink, "Stringfellow," pp. 27-30.

peat, speak the truth." Preaching at its best is precisely such truth-telling in the midst of babel.[42]

This homiletical resistance to the principalities and powers takes two forms: *exposing* the powers of death at work in the world and *envisioning* the alternative of God's redeemed creation. Essential to this twofold resistance is the gift of discernment, the most basic gift of the Holy Spirit to the church, which enables Christians to expose and rebuke the powers of death while also affirming the living, promising Word of God incarnate in the world.[43]

> Discerning signs has to do with comprehending the remarkable in common happenings, with perceiving the saga of salvation within the era of the Fall. It has to do with the ability to interpret ordinary events in both apocalyptic and eschatological connotations, to see portents of death where others find progress or success but, simultaneously, to behold tokens of the reality of the Resurrection or hope where others are consigned to confusion or despair.[44]

On the cross Jesus *exposes* the principalities and powers for what they are — not the divine regents of the world, but rather the violent purveyors of death. In the resurrection Jesus is victorious over the powers of death and gives a *vision* of the promised future, which can be glimpsed even now in the living Word incarnate in the midst of death. The gift of discernment enables Christians to see this crucified and risen Jesus in the world. Preaching that is shaped by the story of Jesus and empowered by the Spirit of discernment will engage in this twofold exposing and envisioning.

In the midst of babel, Christian preaching, first of all, exposes the powers of death. The preacher names the powers and rebukes them. Like the cross of Jesus, this "No!" to the powers, which uncovers their

---

42. In the context of the United States, Stringfellow characterized such truthtelling most basically as interpreting "America biblically," rather than construing "the Bible Americanly" (*An Ethic for Christians*, p. 13). Truthtelling happens when the Bible absorbs the world, rather than vice versa, and when the Word of God is discerned and spoken in the face of death. Like "living humanly," truthtelling is a risky venture.

43. Stringfellow, *An Ethic for Christians*, pp. 138-39.

44. Stringfellow, *An Ethic for Christians*, pp. 138-39.

false claims and deadly lies, marks the beginning of human freedom from the bondage of death.[45] This "No!" takes away the "mirrors" by which the powers delude us into thinking they are the divine regents of the world. The powers are exposed as emperors without any clothes, a disarming humiliation for those who rely so heavily on their pretensions of dignity and control. Indeed, such disarming portends the ultimate defeat of the powers by Jesus. As the writer of Colossians puts it, on the cross Jesus "disarmed the rulers and authorities and made a public example of them, triumphing over them."[46]

Preachers may expose the powers in numerous ways, though a couple of examples will have to suffice here. First, the principalities may be exposed by direct, concrete speech, which cuts through the distortions of babel. In a sermon during the Gulf War, for example, Michael Baxter, a Roman Catholic priest, proclaimed,

> The church demands that Catholics not rally around their leaders once war is waged. . . . What the church fears in this time of war is our complacency. The church fears our instinct to follow the herd, to march in lockstep with whoever is in charge. . . . The church fears that we will, in these times, become so American that we will cease to be Catholic, to be followers of Christ. . . . The church fears that we will lose our vocation.[47]

In the midst of the diversions, deceit, and idolatry of the nation, Baxter exposed the powers of death that would hold Christians captive, and he called the church back to its vocation of resistance. At times, such direct, concrete, truthful speech is required amidst the deadly babel of the world. Too often, however, such speech is missing from the pulpit.

Walter Wink has suggested a second way of exposing the powers, one drawn from Jesus' own Sermon on the Mount: burlesque. Because the powers stand on their dignity, nothing disempowers them more quickly than burlesque or lampooning.[48] In his interpretation of Matthew 5:40, Wink notes the burlesque character of Jesus'

45. Stringfellow, *An Ethic for Christians*, pp. 155-56.
46. Colossians 2:15. See Wink, *Naming*, pp. 55-60; John Howard Yoder, *The Politics of Jesus* (Grand Rapids: Eerdmans, 1972), pp. 147-50.
47. Quoted in *The National Catholic Reporter*, January 31, 1997, p. 6.
48. Wink, *Engaging*, p. 179.

command to "give your inner garment also."[49] The situation is one in which the economic powers have so milked the poor that all they have left to be sued for are their garments. When their outer garment is claimed in court, Wink argues, Jesus counsels them to give the inner one also. That is, the victim of the economic system, who has no other recourse, takes off the inner garment and walks out of the court stark naked. In this way the victim not only retains his or her status as a moral agent, but also unmasks the system's essential cruelty and "burlesques its pretensions to justice, law, and order."[50] As the person walks out of court naked and people on the streets begin to ask what is going on, the economic system itself stands naked and is exposed for what it is — a system that treats the poor as "sponge[s] to be squeezed dry by the rich."[51] By presenting this ethical option in his sermon, Jesus himself actually engages in a homiletical burlesque of the economic system.

Such a comic and burlesque style can be a powerful way to expose the powers. Through the use of risky humor, preaching may unfold the logical consequences of the way of the powers and thereby unmask them for what they are, burst their pretentious bubbles, and free worshipers from their tyranny. Rather than somber, self-important sermons dealing with such matters as capitalism or individualism, preachers from time to time may offer startlingly comic or burlesque depictions of the powers, lampooning the absurdity of their claims. Then a space may be created for the redemptive power of the Word, not just for the hearers, but for the powers themselves.[52]

Whether through direct speech or through other, more creative approaches, preachers confronting the powers will find ways to expose them. At times such resistance will indeed seem fragile, puny, and foolish. At other times, the preacher will meet with opposition or create conflict. At all times, such preaching will require imagination

49. Wink, *Engaging*, pp. 177-79. See also Walter Wink, "Neither Passivity nor Violence: Jesus' Third Way," *Forum* 7 (March/June 1991): 12.

50. Wink, "Jesus' Third Way," p. 12.

51. Wink, "Jesus' Third Way," p. 12.

52. Because the powers are not destroyed or violently overthrown, the possibility is opened for their redemption, their return to the good purposes for which they were created. See Wink, "Jesus' Third Way," p. 12. Stringfellow also hopes for the redemption of the powers. See, for example, *Free in Obedience*, p. 73.

and courage. Nevertheless, the vocation of the preacher as a "keeper of the Word" is to speak the truth and expose the powers. In the midst of babel, such truthtelling is essential for the life of the church and the redemption of the world.

A second way preachers resist the powers is by envisioning the redeemed creation, which may be glimpsed now wherever "tokens of the Resurrection" are discerned in the fallen world. In these moments, which often come as surprising gifts, preachers may discern in the midst of death the "Word of God indwelling in all Creation and transfiguring common history. . . ."[53] Whereas the first form of resistance, like the cross, exposes the powers of death, this second form of resistance "exposes" the victory of the resurrected Jesus over death.

Not long ago, Will Willimon wrote, "Our greatest ethical, political need right now is not for new or better rules. What we're dying of is a lack of imagination."[54] This second form of resistance involves precisely that kind of imagination; it involves envisioning an alternative world to the world of death that would hold us captive.

Such preaching can involve daring visions indeed, as the Bible reminds us: "The wolf shall live with the lamb . . ." (Isaiah 11:6). "Blessed are you who are poor, for yours is the kingdom of God" (Luke 6:20). "They will not hurt or destroy on all my holy mountain" (Isaiah 11:9). "Then I saw a new heaven and a new earth" (Revelation 21:1). Such extravagant visions can be a powerful form of resistance, for as Walter Wink has reminded us, "nothing is more revolutionary than a transformation of the fundamental metaphors by which we apprehend the world."[55] In a similar vein, Walter Brueggemann has affirmed, "The poet/prophet is a voice that shatters settled reality and evokes new possibility in the . . . assembly. Preaching continues that dangerous, indispensable habit of speech. The poetic speech of text and . . . sermon is a prophetic construal of a world beyond the one taken for granted."[56]

Two years ago, shortly after Labor Day, I was standing on a plat-

53. Stringfellow, *An Ethic for Christians*, p. 139.

54. William H. Willimon, "Christian Ethics: When the Personal Is Public Is Cosmic," *Theology Today* 52 (October 1995): 373.

55. Wink, *Engaging*, p. 142.

56. Walter Brueggemann, *Finally Comes the Poet: Daring Speech for Proclamation* (Minneapolis: Fortress Press, 1989), p. 4.

form waiting for a subway train in Atlanta. As I was waiting, a homeless man I had met hailed me from across the platform and came to stand with me. He reminded me of his name, Michael (like the angel), and we struck up a conversation. Michael told me about his ongoing search for a job and gave thanks for the many ways God was caring for him. When the train arrived, we boarded, sat down together, and continued our conversation.

At one point I asked Michael where he had eaten lunch on Labor Day — a difficult day for homeless people in Atlanta because many of the services are closed. He told me he had eaten lunch at "910" (which serves lunch to about four hundred people each Labor Day). Michael's eyes widened as he described the large helpings of "real pinto beans" and the generous portions of corn bread — "this thick," he showed me, holding his thumb and forefinger about two inches apart. When he paused, I asked him how many people were at the meal. He stared at me for a moment, and then announced in a loud voice for everyone to hear: "Thousands! There were thousands! They came from the north and the south and the east and the west. There were thousands!"

In the midst of the social and moral death that is homelessness, Michael had discerned the great Messianic Banquet in pinto beans and corn bread shared among poor people. In the grip of principalities and powers that demean and scapegoat the homeless, Michael had discerned an empowering, liberating, eucharistic "token of the Resurrection." And he held that token before me as a vision of God's redeemed creation, when all God's children will eat together in Shalom and the whole creation will rejoice. Michael proclaimed the Word, exposed the authority of Christ over death,[57] and reminded me of the politics of the Eucharist; he brought together Word and sacrament in the doxological vision that lies at the heart of Christian worship — and Christian preaching. And as he spoke in that crowded subway car, the powers were put in their place, and we were set free, even if only for a moment, from the bondage of death.

57. Stringfellow, *Free in Obedience*, p. 72.

Preaching with Hope

Such discernment of "tokens of the Resurrection" in a world of death is a locus of Christian hope, which, in Stringfellow's words, "is reliance upon grace in the face of death; . . . [it] is living constantly, patiently, expectantly, resiliently, joyously in the efficacy of the Word of God."[58] According to Stringfellow, however, genuine hope is known only in the face of death: "Any so-called hope is delusory and false without or apart from the confrontation with the power of death, whatever momentary or circumstantial form that may have."[59] Hope, Stringfellow reminds us, looks for the resurrection in the shadow of the cross. Hope wears a black dress and stands beside a freshly dug grave in the cemetery. Hope stands in line for a bowl of soup with tired, dirty homeless people. Hope plays in housing projects contaminated with lead poisoning. Hope sits in a cell on death row and lies in a bed in a hospice. As Jürgen Moltmann put it, "The messianic hope was never the hope of the victors and the rulers. It was always the hope of the defeated and the ground down."[60] Here is the fundamental tension at the heart of Stringfellow's work: radical hope in the efficacy of the Word amidst unflinching realism about the reality of death. Only as these two are held together will preachers genuinely proclaim the Word of hope.

This tension between the power of hope and the reality of death cannot be faithfully respected by any mere homiletical technique. The two can only be joined in the life of the preacher as a "keeper of the Word." In order to preach *about* hope or *for* hope, preachers must first of all preach *with* hope; they must preach as persons of hope. Such preaching requires of the preacher both an immersion in the memories and promises of the Bible and a life of engagement with the powers of death. Hope-filled preaching that is not delusory or false is possible only when preachers live with the Bible in those places where death seems to reign. In those places of death hope may joyously surprise us, as Michael surprised me on the subway car. In those places of death, the song of hope will also take on new and rich tones.

58. Stringfellow, *An Ethic for Christians*, p. 138.
59. Stringfellow, *An Ethic for Christians*, p. 138.
60. Jürgen Moltmann, *The Way of Jesus Christ: Christology in Messianic Dimensions*, trans. Margaret Kohl (San Francisco: HarperSanFrancisco, 1990), p. 13.

In the places of death the song of hope, first of all, takes on a tone of urgency, which so desperately needs to be heard in comfortable, complacent, middle-class churches. In the grip of the powers there is no time for theories or abstractions or speculations. "I hope God will get me through another night on the streets." "I hope I will not be shot while walking to school." "I hope I will live until my grandchild is born." "I hope I will make it through the day without drugs or alcohol." Preachers learn the urgency of hope in the places of death.

In those places hope also becomes deep. Clichés and shallow optimism won't do. Hope rather takes on the tone of lament: "How long, O Lord? How long?" And hope can sound like anger — anger at the powers of death that crush people every day. Hope, finally, becomes hope in God because the false hopes of human progress and human systems have been stripped away. The promises of the powers have been seen for what they are — the beacons of death, not life, of despair, not hope. In the confrontation with death, hope becomes deep — or it dies.

In the midst of death, hope also becomes broad. Among the poor and the suffering, hope for our own security and well-being is exposed as shallow and inadequate. In those places we discover with the writer of Ephesians that "we are not struggling against the enemies of blood and flesh, but against the rulers, against the authorities, against the cosmic powers, against the spiritual forces of evil" — against the principalities and powers (Ephesians 6:12). In the soup kitchen line, in the prisons, in the barrios or the projects, hope becomes hope for a new order, hope for a new heaven and a new earth, hope for the Messianic Banquet, hope for the reign of God in all its political and social dimensions. Only this kind of hope is broad enough in the face of the powers.

For many of us, such a grand hope is inseparable from grief. For the new age comes only when the present age dies, and many of us enjoy great privilege in the present age. For those of us who are wealthy and powerful, hope for a new creation brings grief over the death of the old world from which we have benefited so much. Resurrection comes only on the other side of crucifixion, and that is painful for those of us who seem to have much to lose. Preaching with hope entails bringing this grief to speech.[61]

61. See Walter Brueggemann, *The Prophetic Imagination* (Philadelphia: Fortress Press, 1978), pp. 44-61, 80-95.

Finally, in the places of death, hope itself becomes a form of resistance — a defiance of the present age and the status quo. Before the powers, hope cannot remain a passive, wishful longing for a better day. Rather, it takes the form of resistance to the principalities that masquerade as common sense; it challenges the closed definitions of reality that offer no alternative future. Confronting the principalities and powers with the resurrection of Jesus, the Word of hope ultimately frees people to live humanly in the face of death.[62]

62. A different version of this essay by Chuck Campbell appeared as "Principalities, Powers, and Preaching: Learning from William Stringfellow" in *Interpretation* 51 (October 1997): 384-401.

Unmasked

In Colossians 2:15, we read that on the cross Jesus "disarmed the principalities and powers and made a public example of them, triumphing over them." This text provides a profound social and political understanding of Jesus' death on the cross. On the cross Jesus deals decisively with the large and powerful social realities — institutions, corporations, bureaucracies, ideologies, states, governments — that actively and aggressively shape our world and our lives.

In his life and ministry, Jesus engaged and challenged these powers. He lived free from their clutches and embodied an alternative to their spirit of survival, domination, and death. And, of course, the powers couldn't stand such a challenge, so they nailed him to the cross. However, on the cross, Jesus unmasks the powers by bringing their true nature to light. Jesus reveals the powers for what they are — not the representatives of God (despite their idolatrous claims), and not the agents of life, but rather the opponents of God and the purveyors of death. By unmasking the powers, Jesus also *disarms* them; he takes away the "mirrors" by which they maintain the illusion that they are indeed the divine regents of the world. And once the powers are unmasked and disarmed, we are set free from their clutches. The powers can no longer fool us with their promises and claims, for we have seen them for what they are. On the cross Jesus liberates humanity from our enslavement to the powers.

In a similar way, Martin Luther King, Jr., exposed and disarmed the powers of racism through his nonviolent campaigns. When the white "powers that be" turned hoses and dogs on the marchers — and the images were splashed across TV — the reality of racism was graphically and publicly exposed for everyone to see. And King knew just what he was doing: "Let them get their dogs," he shouted, "and let them get the hose, and we will leave them standing before their God and the world spattered with the blood and reeking with the stench of their Negro brothers." It is necessary, he continued, "to bring these issues to the surface, to bring them out into the open where everybody can see them."[1] And once exposed by King in this way, racism began to lose some of its power over many of us. King helps us understand what happened on the cross. Jesus graphically exposed the powers for what they are and left them spattered with his blood. And by exposing them, Jesus disarmed them; he triumphed over them and freed us from their grip.

During a recent reflection time following the Butler Street Breakfast, Ed Loring commented that homeless people play a similar role in our society. Like Jesus and Martin Luther King, Jr., they unmask the principalities and powers, exposing them as powers of death. Ed's comment came and went quickly, but I have been thinking about it for several weeks, and I believe his insight helps us grasp both the theological significance of homeless people and the reasons for the current attacks upon them.

Homeless people — the visible poor, as one author has called them[2] — do indeed unmask the deadly principalities and powers at work in our society. Seeing a homeless person asleep on the concrete or arrested for urinating in public or standing in line for a bowl of grits, we witness in a stark way the deadly realities and consequences of our competitive, greed-driven capitalist economy. We see that our economic system — both the institutions that embody it and the spirit that drives it — promises us life and prosperity, but in reality leads to suffering and death. Homeless people in our society embody the way of the cross; through their public suffering, they remove the scales from our eyes and expose the lies of the powers that promise us life, but lure us into the ways of death.

---

1. Quoted in Richard Lischer, *The Preacher King: Martin Luther King, Jr. and the Word That Moved America* (New York: Oxford University Press, 1995), p. 157.

2. Joel Blau, *The Visible Poor: Homelessness in the United States* (New York: Oxford University Press, 1992; Oxford University paperback, 1993).

So it is no wonder that the political and economic powers are doing everything they can to crucify homeless people — to remove them from downtown and keep them out of sight. This is exactly what we would expect the powers to do with those who uncover their lies and expose their deadly ways. For the "powers that be," homeless people are not simply unsightly or troublesome. Rather, people who live on the streets are threatening at a much deeper level: they expose the greed and oppression at the heart of our society and leave those in power spattered with their blood. They reveal the "powers that be" as the purveyors of death, rather than the agents of life. So we should not be surprised when the powers, wishing to maintain the illusion of their righteousness, seek to remove homeless people from the city — just as Jesus was crucified outside the city.

Homeless people perform a critical theological function in our society: they unmask the deadly ways of the powers by embodying the realities and consequences of our economic system. This is why it is so important for middle-class folks to spend time with people who live on the streets: our own freedom — our very life — depends on it. Once we have spent time with homeless people, once we have heard their stories and seen their suffering, we can no longer be fooled by the "powers that be." We can no longer be deluded by urban camping laws or "quality of life" ordinances. For we begin to see clearly that the issue isn't "quality of life," but the delusions of death. Standing before the cross of the homeless person, we see the powers for what they are — not the agents of life, but the purveyors of death — and we are set free from our own captivity to their false claims and deadly lies. We are set free to weep over the suffering, to confess our own complicity, and to resist the ways of death.[3] And that freedom is a gift of grace from our brothers and sisters who live on the streets.[4]

---

3. For the sequence from weeping to confession to resistance, I am grateful to Christine M. Smith, *Preaching as Weeping, Confession, and Resistance: Radical Responses to Radical Evil* (Louisville: Westminster/John Knox Press, 1992).

4. This essay by Chuck Campbell originally appeared in *Hospitality* 17 (May 1998): 1.

Street Readings/Reading the Streets:
Reading the Bible Through
the Lens of the Streets,
Reading the Streets Through
the Lens of the Bible

When most people imagine what it's like to interpret Scripture, the primary image likely to come to mind is of the pastor or scholar, a monklike figure, toiling hour after hour in the solitude of the study, surrounded by more large, dusty books than most people would wish to see in a lifetime. While reality is usually not quite so harsh, the image of books and solitude is not off the mark. Biblical interpretation as it is usually practiced today is a personal skill, nurtured in libraries and studies, consisting of a diverse array of reading strategies designed to elicit informed, critical engagement with the text — that is, to "lead meaning out of" (exegete) the text. Thus, we train pastors to use the best available commentaries and lexicons, alongside the occasional critical article, in order to bring forth the message(s) of the text for the sake of the congregation.

The model of the individual interpreter in the study has served us well and will undoubtedly continue to do so for generations to come. But it does have limitations. Recently, for example, we have begun to rediscover the importance of reading and interpreting Scripture in more communal settings, such as the congregation, where diverse voices can enter the interpretive fray.[1] The congregation is a different social setting from the pastor's study, and can generate a different level and character of engagement with the text. In Biblical studies we have also determined the importance of social reality in the interpretive process. We know both that the world of the Bible is not the same as our own and that we must discern the differences and own the gaps as fully as we can. We also know that our own "social location," the fact that I am a white, middle-class male, for example, powerfully shapes how and what we see when we read Scripture. As in real estate, so also in the interpretation of Scripture, the most important principles are location, location, location.

The Importance of Physical Location

Discussion of the importance of location in biblical interpretation, however, has focused on "social" location to the virtual exclusion of physical location. "Social location" itself is usually articulated in terms of elements of our personal identity, especially race, gender, and socioeconomic status. But these elements of "social location" take on different priority and meaning in the different physical locations through which we move in life. Thus, if social location plays a crucial role in the interpretation of Scripture, then so do the physical settings in which we read.

Social philosophers and critics have in recent years explored the ways in which our physical arrangements of space represent and reflect our social values and priorities, as well as the ways in which even

---

1. See, for example, Stephen E. Fowl and L. Gregory Jones, *Reading in Communion: Scripture and Ethics in Christian Life* (Grand Rapids: Eerdmans, 1991). We have concurrently begun to acknowledge the importance of the congregation in proclamation, even asserting that preaching is a genuinely communal art. See Lucy Atkinson Rose, *Sharing the Word: Preaching in the Roundtable Church* (Louisville: Westminster/John Knox Press, 1997); John S. McClure, *The Roundtable Pulpit: Where Leadership and Preaching Meet* (Nashville: Abingdon Press, 1995). But if we are to make real headway in realizing the missionary dimensions of the Christian life, we must also reclaim the world around us as a right and proper locus for both interpretation and proclamation.

our perception of physical space — our capacity for "sight," that is — is culturally determined.[2] Students of the Bible ought therefore to give attention not only to our "social location" as we read texts, but to our physical locations as well. More concretely, what if we were to move our engagement with Scripture even beyond the typical settings of church life and into the worlds where people live and work each day? The recovery of missionary vision and vitality in North American churches may require just such a move.

It does not take much effort to realize the powerful impact of our physical and social setting on what and how we read, even on how we feel about it. Most of us do not feel much discomfort reading the Bible in church on Sunday morning, but we may experience acute embarrassment about the prospect of reading the Bible at the mall or in the workplace. For mainstream Christians, in other words, biblical interpretation is a practice at home in the confines of the church and its official spaces, but not necessarily in the public sphere. Even within the church itself, physical setting determines how one reads. In the library or the pastor's study, for example, one's primary conversation partners will be the learned scholars, for better or worse. At the desk, interpretation is more likely to be constrained by the limits of one's own imagination, or by whatever other book is open at the moment. And in the private study it is all too easy to limit our engagement with God's Word to the world of words. Perhaps the level of abstraction that seems to cloak much of our official exegesis and theology is a function of the physical settings in which we typically conduct our most serious engagements with the Bible.

One of our first efforts to facilitate an engagement between theological education and the world of the Open Door Community took place in a classroom at Columbia Seminary. We had invited Ed Loring, C. M. Sherman, and Ron Jackson from the Open Door to join us in

---

2. See, for example, Edward T. Hall, *The Hidden Dimension* (New York: Doubleday, 1966); Henri Lefebvre, *The Production of Space* (Oxford and Cambridge, Mass.: Blackwell, 1991); Edward W. Soja, *Thirdspace: Journeys to Los Angeles and Other Real-and-Imagined Places* (Oxford and Cambridge, Mass.: Blackwell, 1996); Derek Gregory, *Geographical Imaginations* (Oxford and Cambridge, Mass.: Blackwell, 1994); David Harvey, *The Condition of Postmodernity* (Oxford and Cambridge, Mass.: Blackwell, 1990) and *Justice, Nature and the Geography of Difference* (Oxford and Cambridge, Mass.: Blackwell, 1996).

reading and discussing Mark's Gospel. From the start it was evident that the "worlds" we brought with us to the classroom generated different readings of the text. Broadly speaking, the members of the Open Door were much more willing to embrace the apocalyptic dimensions of Mark's Gospel than were the majority of the (middle-class) seminary students. The Open Door folks were also more willing to take seriously what Mark had to say, for example, about riches and poverty, or "losing one's life in order to save it." In our discussions of suffering, however, the tensions became irreconcilable. As Ed noted almost immediately, talk of suffering took on a distinctly abstract tone in the context of the seminary classroom, far removed from the immediacy, reality, and urgency of suffering that one could encounter every day on the streets of Atlanta. Our subsequent move to the streets as the primary location for our interpretation of Scripture emerged directly from the tensions and frustrations of these conversations.

If one of the goals of exegesis is to teach folks to read the Bible "in context," we need to consider seriously the use of spaces other than the traditional classroom. We know from the cognitive sciences that human learning is deeply influenced — and sometimes limited — by the physical space and conditions in which that learning happens. Most of us in the United States grew up doing our "official" learning within the physical and social space of the classroom, where both students and faculty usually know what patterns of discourse and social interaction are appropriate. So when we read the Bible in the classrooms of our seminaries and churches, the physical space itself often may function as a domesticating and confining force — a way of preserving the comfortably abstract character of much of our reflection and discourse.

When we read the Bible with our classes on the streets of Atlanta, we use the same methodological tools we do in classrooms at the seminary. The only difference is the physical space itself, and our usually heightened sensitivities. The sights, sounds, smells, social arrangements, and experiences form the canvas for our engagement with the text. The principle is simple: where we learn shapes what we learn, and where we read shapes how we read.

Catalyzing Scripture and Context

On the streets the descriptive and evocative power of the biblical text seems more obvious, vibrant, and powerful than in the classroom. This is so for two reasons. First, the physical context of the streets helps us see things in the text in fresh ways, raising different issues and questions, or raising them with different immediacy and priority. This becomes especially clear for students who have already worked on a passage in another context. One of our students, Rachel Winter, had preached during a summer internship at a congregation in Birmingham on Mark's version of the Gerasene demoniac (Mark 5:1-20). During the Fall semester, she preached again on the same text, this time after serving for eight weeks at the Butler Street Breakfast, after spending twenty-four hours on the streets, and after participating in several worship gatherings with homeless people, in which Scripture was read and proclaimed. "I've seen this passage in a new light," she said as she began her second sermon on this passage, "and I've thought about it in ways I've never thought about it before. My interpretation may not be the most 'accurate' one, but it comes from my experience working with the homeless." She went on to note the ways in which her experiences among homeless people and her grappling with Mark 5 had opened up a distinctive perspective on the powers, "both the saving powers and the controlling and demonic powers at work in the world." Rachel's physical location, and her heightened awareness of her social location, had a clear impact on her understanding of the text. The context of the streets, and our worship alongside the people who live there, had generated a distinctive engagement with the Scriptures.

Second, the biblical text, as Rachel's story also illustrates, helps us read our context in different ways. The Scriptures unmask the truth about the world around us, especially when the world and the text are clearly juxtaposed. William Stringfellow, the lay theologian whose engagement with Scripture also was rooted in his experience on the streets, was aware that in contexts of oppression, suffering, and death, reading Scripture not only unmasks reality but is an act of resistance.[3]

---

3. Bill Wylie Kellermann, ed., *A Keeper of the Word: Selected Writings of William Stringfellow* (Grand Rapids: Eerdmans, 1994), pp. 173-74.

Even where oppression, suffering, and death are not immediately evident, reading Scripture opens our eyes to discern anew aspects of our experience that we might otherwise take for granted. Most of our students, for example, have at one time or another visited many of the places we usually take our classes in downtown Atlanta, but in the social role of a shopper, a tourist, or a visitor to one of Atlanta's entertainment or athletic venues. When we experience these same spaces with the Scriptures open, we "see" them differently, as the following story illustrates.

One Thursday morning in October, after serving breakfast at Butler Street C.M.E. Church, our class headed downtown for our time of Bible study and reflection. Our group was a bit smaller than usual that day: five students, a faculty person, and Tonnie King from the Open Door. After walking several blocks we arrived at our destination, the tall bank building that sits across the street to the east of Woodruff Park. We formed a small circle, down the steps and several yards away from the entrance to the bank, spreading our backpacks, our notebooks, and our Bibles about us on the ground. We were not trying to draw attention to ourselves; we just wanted to use this space in the heart of Atlanta's business district in a new way. The focus passage for the morning was James 5:1-6.

Here, in a blistering critique of wealth, James warns the rich of the judgment about to come upon them (5:1-3). Rather than share their resources with the poor, the rich have let their accumulated wealth sit idle; they have "laid up treasure for the last days." But now it is corroded and tarnished — and its rustiness will serve as evidence against them (vv. 2-3). Verse 4 makes clear that the wealth of the rich has been acquired by injustice, by depriving the poor of their just wages. The Lord of Hosts now hears the cries of the harvesters, the typical day laborers of the first-century world. The rich do not hear their cries. Preoccupied and heedless of God, like pigs at the trough, they have "fattened their hearts in a day of slaughter" (5:5). What is more, the rich are guilty of judicial murder, using the machinery of justice to condemn and kill the righteous (5:6). In a telling final comment, James notes that the poor offer no resistance.

Kazy Blocher, the student who was leading our reflections for the morning, distributed slips of paper to each of us, each slip naming a particular person we would likely find working, doing business in, or loitering around the bank. Using some imaginative role play we were to consider how each of these people — tellers, customers, executives, security guards, and the homeless people across the street from us in Woodruff Park — would understand and respond to this passage from James. We didn't have to work very hard — we could see the modern-day equivalents of the people described in James 5:1-6, including ourselves, all around us.

After a few minutes of conversation, we were approached by a security guard from the bank (and soon after by another guard and a supervisor), who wanted to know who we were and what we were doing there. Though sitting in a very public place some distance away from the bank entrance, we apparently posed a threat. We identified ourselves, telling the guard that we were there for a Bible study about rich people, and invited him to join us. Disarmed (though still "armed") by the invitation, he turned back and spoke to his supervisor, then turned again to listen to our conversation. After a minute or two, he identified himself as a Christian. "How do you like working in the bank?" we asked. "It's a good place to work, and I thank the Lord that I have a job," he told us, noting that the people in the bank were usually very nice. Then he excused himself to return to his work, adding that the bank didn't often have groups that sat on the steps for Bible study.

As we continued our discussion that morning, we remarked that the perspective of our security guard was not unlike the righteous poor described in James 5. Though not employed in a particularly well paying profession, he was grateful to God for all he did have, and he was probably neither willing nor in a position to offer "resistance" to the rich people using his bank. Like most Christians in this culture, and like most of us gathered on the steps of the bank that day, the security guard accepted his lot in life probably as a "natural" expression of the economy, and even as a "God-given" reality. His gratitude to God was a wonderful expression of his faith. But his, and our, willingness to go along and get along with the social and economic arrangement dictated to us by the powers of this world is precisely what James is attacking so vociferously.

Reading James 5 on the steps of the bank in the middle of Atlanta's tall buildings raised for us several questions we might otherwise not have considered. Does the seductiveness of wealth in modern capitalism, as in the patronage-based economy of the first century, manifest itself in our deference toward and emulation of the rich? Does the rapidly growing disparity between the fabulously rich and the desperately poor have anything to do with what James describes? Are today's poor deprived of their fair wages? Do the rich use the courts and the justice system to their advantage? Are we, like the rich in James, comfortably preoccupied — by television and the entertainment culture, for example — and heedless of God's warnings? When James describes the righteous one who offers no resistance, is this to praise such behavior, or simply to describe the way the world works?

In short, the Scriptures are an indispensable resource for "reading the streets," but they work most effectively in this regard, and thereby offer us the most powerful tools for resistance, when we actually read *on* the streets.

The Biblical Precedent for Public Interpretation

While the first Christians, like us, relied upon the resources of gifted teachers and usually followed the interpretive traditions of their day, their interpretive practices apparently differed from ours with regard to physical setting. Not only did they read and interpret the Scriptures in their eucharistic assemblies (which may have been more "public" than our typical worship services[4]), they also excelled at interpreting Scripture in the public places where they discerned the Spirit of God at work. Jesus is portrayed in the Gospels as interpreting Israel's Scriptures not only in the synagogue, but in the town streets, in the fields, on the mountains and seas, in houses and on highways. And the early Christians followed his lead. One of the first recorded instances of "Christian" interpretation of Scripture is found in Acts 8, where Philip, a deacon in the Jerusalem Church, "guides" the Ethiopian eunuch in a reading of Isaiah — while riding in a chariot (Acts 8:27-39)! The apostle Paul did some of his finest interpretive work while in prison. More-

---

4. While modern North Americans consider the house a private sphere, the ancient household was a decidedly public place, where even uninvited guests and strangers could observe first-hand what was happening. Knowing this reality helps us make sense of such texts as 1 Corinthians 14:23-24.

over, throughout the Gospels and Acts we see countless occasions in which the interpretation of Scripture takes place in conjunction with public events. Luke presents Peter's sermon at Pentecost (Acts 2), for example, as if there was little or no time for exegetical preparation. The pouring out of the Spirit upon the gathered Christians was a public event that required immediate explanation in order to contradict the onlookers' initial explanation that the disciples were merely drunk. In this instance, Scripture and public events were mutually interpretive, each illuminating the other.

If we are to take seriously the public dimension of interpretation that we find in the pages of the Bible itself, we will need to consider moving our primary training grounds for interpretation from the classroom to the places where people live — homes, businesses, executive parks, malls, and the streets. If biblical interpretation is to have vitality and power in relation to the social structures, economic systems, and political institutions of our own day, it must be set free from the social and spatial confinements imposed by the academy and the structures of the institutional church. We must learn to read the Bible in new places!

None of this is to suggest that we abandon libraries, studies, and classrooms, or in any way diminish the use of sound exegetical methods and tools as we engage in the interpretation of Scripture. Nor is it to suggest that we do not read the Bible well or faithfully in the guild or the congregation. The seminary campus and the church building are among the places where God is at work. But they are surely not the only places. We need to ask, then, not only how we ought to read the Bible (usually addressed by questions of method), but *where* and *with whom*.

Reading the Scriptures on the streets has convinced us that the Bible can be powerfully and faithfully read and proclaimed in the places where our sight is filled with the distorting, idolatrous, corrosive images of worldly power and wealth. Here the gospel most desperately needs to be heard. Here the reading of Scripture not only offers us the tools of resistance, but leads us toward faithful embodiment and performance, the culmination of genuine interpretation.[5]

---

5. Written for this volume by Stan Saunders.

Street Preaching

On a Thursday morning in November, 1996, Melanie Mitchell, a student at Columbia Theological Seminary, was scheduled to preach on the streets for the first time — a required (and dreaded) assignment in the course, "Good News to the Poor." Following the Butler Street Breakfast, she would preach on the sidewalk outside the church among a group of homeless people and Open Door volunteers who gathered for worship every Thursday morning on the corner of Butler Street and Coca-Cola Place. Following her sermon, the homeless men and women would critique her preaching.

Melanie didn't sleep much the night before she preached. And during the breakfast that morning she was nervous and preoccupied, going over and over her sermon in her mind. (After all, you can't use a manuscript when preaching on the streets!) "I felt nauseous," she later commented. With the support of her classmates, however, she made it through the morning. Finally, the moment came, and she stepped out onto the sidewalk with Bible in hand, scared half to death. She led us in prayer and then, with cars honking in the background and pedestrians walking all around her, Melanie preached from Isaiah 11:1-10. And she preached with a passion and energy that surprised everyone, including herself. When she was finished, she sat down with an expression of both relief and wonder. "I did that?" her face seemed to be saying. "Wow!" everyone exclaimed. "We've never seen that side of you." "What happened?" "You were amazing!" Somehow, the street had freed Melanie to preach in a way she had never before imagined.

As she later wrote to her boyfriend,

> I preached on the street today. It was exhilarating. . . . I had to shout because of the noise on the street, and the best thing was that I would ask questions and the people would answer: "Does God want people to go hungry?" "No!!" "Does God judge people by the clothes they wear?" "No!!" I would make statements, "Jesus will rule with justice!" and they would respond saying, "Amen!" . . . And it was fun. The Bible is amazing because I would really be scared if I had to stand up and speak without it. Also, if it weren't for the Spirit I could not have preached because I was so scared. As soon as I prayed and began reading I was fine. Afterwards, when people were giving feedback I became myself again and began to blush and giggle. But when I was preaching I was able to be bold and passionate. . . .

Later in the letter she returned to the subject:

> I wanted to say something else about the sermon. What you might be able to relate to is the challenge of doing something that scares you to death — like skiing on a steep slope, or hang-gliding, or bungee-jumping, or anything that involves a risk. When you are able to do it, you feel exhilarated because a challenge has been met; the obstacle of fear has been overcome. Have you ever experienced that?

On that Thursday morning in November, Melanie Mitchell joined a great cloud of witnesses who have taken the Word to the streets.

A Long and Lively Tradition

When the Day of Pentecost had come, the disciples were gathered in one place. A rush of wind filled the house and tongues of fire rested on everyone. All were filled with the Spirit and began to speak in other languages. At this strange outbreak of the Spirit, Jews from all the nations gathered outside the house where the disciples were staying.

Then Peter went out to the street, "raised his voice," and boldly proclaimed the gospel to the crowd.[1]

The church reads and remembers this familiar story annually on the Day of Pentecost. We celebrate the coming of the Spirit, the birth of the church, the breaking down of barriers between peoples, the reversal of Babel (Genesis 11:1-9). As we celebrate Pentecost inside our festively decorated sanctuaries, however, we may easily overlook one aspect of the story. From the beginning, the church's preaching was a missional act directed beyond the walls of the sanctuary to the surrounding culture(s). And, though it may cause many of us some discomfort, the initial form of the church's missional proclamation was *street preaching*.[2]

Peter's street sermon on Pentecost, moreover, is consistent with the rest of the biblical witness. Much of the preaching in the Bible takes place "in the streets," in public places where people gather. Prior to Pentecost, street preaching had a long and rich history. The prophets of Israel proclaimed the Word of the Lord and performed their sign acts "on the streets." Jonah, in particular, might be the paradigmatic missionary street preacher, walking through the entire city of Nineveh reluctantly proclaiming his message of repentance. And Jesus followed in the prophets' footsteps. While he certainly preached in the temple and in homes, Jesus also regularly spoke in public places, including the streets and markets, where people gathered. After Pentecost, the tradition continued, as Paul became possibly the most effective street preacher in the history of the church. Whether because they were not always welcome in traditional meeting places or because they sensed the missional drive of the gospel or because they announced the public

1. Although Acts 2 doesn't explicitly state that Peter and the disciples went outside to the street, the text requires this interpretation. The number of people who had gathered could not possibly have fit into the house (see vv. 5-6, and v. 41). In addition, the emphasis on Peter's standing with the other disciples and "raising his voice" points in this direction (v. 14). The clear implication is that at some point Peter and the disciples went outside to the street to "address the crowd."

2. By "street preaching" I mean preaching that goes out to people in public spaces, rather than waiting for people to come to the preacher. I thus am not referring to all "open-air" preaching, some of which relies on people coming to a designated place to hear a well-known preacher. A Billy Graham crusade, for example, is not "street preaching." And much of the preaching of the Awakenings, although done in the open air, would fall outside this category.

claims of God's Word, the preachers in the Bible didn't wait for people to come to them and hear their proclamation; they instead took the Word to the people on the streets.

In the history of the church, this tradition has been continued — and not just by stereotypical wild-eyed fundamentalists. Through the centuries, street preachers have played a significant role in the renewal of preaching and the reformation of the church. The preaching revival and ecclesial renewal in the thirteenth century, for example, was spearheaded by itinerant street preachers, the most well known among them St. Francis of Assisi. Sounding like a modern Salvation Army group, the Franciscans, when they entered a town or village,

> would sing out their characteristic greeting in the vernacular, much as any traveling chapman or hawker would sing out his wares. The people, eager to hear news, would leave their shops and gather round, conducting them to the market-place, where they would start their hymns and preach their popular sermons.[3]

Later, the forerunners of the Reformation, including "heretics" such as the Lollards and Savonarola, took the Word out of the churches and into the streets.[4] Apparently recognizing the value of this approach, the great Reformer, Martin Luther, reportedly proclaimed one Sunday that preaching should *not* be done inside churches.[5] Two centuries later, George Whitefield, who had worn out his welcome in the established

3. Harold Goad, *Greyfriars: The Story of St. Francis and His Followers* (London: John Westhouse Publishers, 1947), p. 87.

4. Charles H. Spurgeon, "Open-Air Preaching: A Sketch of Its History and Remarks Thereon," p. 1; available from http://biblebelievers.simplenet.com/StreetPreaching2.html; Internet; accessed 25 January 1999. See also John R. Archer, "Wycliffe, John," in *The Concise Encyclopedia of Preaching*, ed. William H. Willimon and Richard Lischer (Louisville: Westminster/John Knox Press, 1995), pp. 514-16.

5. Søren Kierkegaard, *Attack Upon "Christendom,"* trans. Walter Lowrie (Princeton University Press, 1944; Beacon paperback edition, Boston: Beacon Press, 1956), p. viii. Of the Reformation, Spurgeon writes, ". . . where would the Reformation have been if its great preachers had confined themselves to churches and cathedrals? How would the common people have become indoctrinated with the Gospel had it not been for those far-wandering evangelists, the colporteurs, and those daring innovators who found a pulpit on every heap of stones, and an audience chamber in every open space near the abodes of men?" (Spurgeon, "Open-Air Preaching," p. 2).

Church of England, took the gospel outside to the poor, who had been neglected by the church. A new world of possibilities opened on February 17, 1739, when Whitefield first preached to a group of poor colliers among the coal mines in Kingswood near Bristol.

The tradition of street preaching has continued in the United States, from the time Whitefield himself crossed the ocean and preached not only in the fields, but in the public squares of the cities. The ongoing story includes not only the preaching of the Great Awakenings, but the evangelism of the Salvation Army, the virtually unknown Roman Catholic street preachers of the mid-twentieth century, the public sermons of the civil rights movement, the liturgical direct-action campaigns of the anti-nuclear movement, and the countless individual street preachers who have been proclaiming the Word on the street corners of America up to this very moment. Even Dorothy Day understood her Catholic Worker paper to be a way of taking the Word to the streets: "It is easy enough to write and publish a paper and mail it out with the help of volunteers to the four corners of the earth. But it becomes an actual, living thing when you get out on the street corners with the word, as St. Paul did in the early days of Christianity."[6]

Throughout the history of the church certain groups and individuals have grasped the truth of Søren Kierkegaard's words:

> . . . sermons should not be preached in churches. It harms Christianity in a high degree and alters its very nature, that it is brought into an artistic remoteness from reality, instead of being heard in the midst of real life, and that precisely for the sake of the conflict (the collision). For all this talk about quiet, about quiet places and quiet hours, as the right element for Christianity, is absurd.
>
> So then sermons should not be preached in churches but in the street, in the midst of life, of the reality of daily life, weekday life.[7]

Although mainline churches have shown little interest in street preaching, it has been one of the most enduring and vigorous forms of the church's missional proclamation.

6. Dorothy Day, *The Long Loneliness* (1952; repr. San Francisco: HarperSanFrancisco, 1952; reprint, 1981), p. 204.
7. Kierkegaard, *Attack Upon "Christendom,"* p. viii.

Beyond Stereotypes

There is good reason why many Christians are skeptical about street preaching. The current image of street preaching has been shaped by angry, abusive preachers who seek to "save souls" by standing on street corners and shouting vitriolic, judgmental words of "hellfire and damnation." Both the message these preachers proclaim and the way they act hardly seem to deserve the name "gospel." A friend of mine who worked for years in a women's health clinic that performed abortions cringes at the slightest mention of "street preaching." She and her patients endured terrible abuse by preachers who showered them almost daily with threats and hate. She wants nothing more to do with that kind of preaching, and most of us can sympathize with her.

Just because street preaching has been abused, however, is no reason to dismiss it. If that were the case, we would also have to dismiss Sunday morning "pulpit preaching," which has certainly known its share of abuse. Moreover, even a cursory look at the history of street preaching suggests that our contemporary stereotypes are inadequate. Street preaching has not always focused narrowly on "saving souls" and has not always "turned people off" with a hate-filled message. Rather, street preaching has taken a variety of different forms and served a number of different purposes. A brief look at four of these alternatives can broaden our understanding of the Word on the streets.

Reform

Street preaching has frequently arisen at times when the church has grown moribund and in need of reform. Because of hardened or lifeless institutional structures and practices, preachers have taken to the streets as a means of renewing the Body of Christ. The itinerant preaching of St. Francis, for example, was driven by a desire to reform the life of the church. Francis's ministry was shaped by a visitation from the Lord, who spoke to Francis from a cross in the ruined little church of St. Damian outside Assisi: "Francis, go and repair my church which, as you can see, is falling down." This call motivated Francis's preaching.[8] Speaking in a vernacular, extemporaneous style, which often included dramatic gestures, symbolic actions, and simple everyday parables, Francis called people to repentance and new life in ways that were both engaging and popular — even entertaining. In this way, Francis and his followers "brought new life, faith, sentiment, and poetry into the dry or sluggish veins of a too conventional worship."[9]

Similarly, George Whitefield, along with John Wesley, was driven to the streets by the failures of the established Church of England, which had grown out of touch with the common people and had fostered apathy and indifference among large numbers of Christians. Relying on the power of the Word and the movement of the Spirit, rather than on secular laws, social customs, and institutional habits, Whitefield's "street preaching" was a direct challenge to the church. Rejecting classical models of preaching for extemporaneous, dramatic sermons that addressed the passions of his hearers, Whitefield's style itself challenged the institutional pulpit of the Church of England.[10] While definitely seeking to "save souls," Whitefield's larger purpose was the reform of the church.

Reconciliation

One of the most interesting chapters in the history of street preaching took place among Roman Catholics in the United States during the middle part of the twentieth century. At a time of strident anti-Catholicism in the United States, groups of Catholic priests, seminarians, and college women took to the streets to counter Protestant bigotry. Knowing that Protestants would never *voluntarily* visit Catholic churches, where they might learn the truth about Catholicism, members of the Vincentian religious community formed "motor missions" and went out to public places in the rural Midwest to speak with their

8. John R. H. Moorman, *Saint Francis of Assisi* (London: SCM Press, 1950), pp. 19-22.

9. Goad, *Greyfriars*, p. 92.

10. Harry S. Stout, "Whitefield, George," in *The Concise Encyclopedia of Preaching*, ed. William H. Willimon and Richard Lischer (Louisville: Westminster/John Knox Press, 1995), pp. 503-4. In the encyclopedia, see also Ted A. Campbell, "Itinerant and Open-Air Preaching," pp. 274-76.

Protestant neighbors. As one of the organizers of the missions, Lester Fallon, put it, "the street was a place where non-Catholics could be reached."[11]

The purpose of the preaching was "not to convert, but to create an atmosphere of tolerance through a simple, clear, non-argumentative explanation of Catholic beliefs."[12] By speaking face to face with Protestants and distributing literature, the Vincentians hoped to dispel misunderstandings and show people that "their ill-will and prejudice against Catholics and the Catholic Church [were] resting on very poor foundations."[13] While the missions didn't fully alleviate anti-Catholic bigotry, genuine reconciliation did take place. On one occasion, a skeptical Protestant minister came to the preaching and then stayed to talk with the priests for several hours following the formal presentation. As one priest wrote about the Protestant pastor, "He was not nearer to being a Catholic when he left. But he was a friend."[14] On another occasion, following a visit by the street preachers, local Protestants gave money and materials to help a small group of Catholics in the town construct a church.[15] Nothing could seemingly be further from our contemporary stereotypes of street preaching.

Resistance

In the anti-war and anti-nuclear movements, radical Christians have engaged in street preaching to expose and resist the idolatrous powers of the world that challenge the Lordship of Jesus Christ. This kind of

11. Douglas J. Slawson, "Thirty Years of Street Preaching: Vincentian Motor Missions, 1934-1965," *Church History* 62 (1993): 64.

12. Slawson, "Thirty Years of Street Preaching," p. 64.

13. Slawson, "Thirty Years of Street Preaching," p. 79. The Vincentians were not the only street preachers in the Roman Catholic Church at that time. David Goldstein and Martha Moore Avery (both laypeople) organized the Catholic Truth Guild, which later became the Catholic Campaigners for Christ. Having a more evangelistic and social purpose, Goldstein and Avery preached about the bearing of Catholicism on contemporary issues and events. See Debra Campbell, "A Catholic Salvation Army: David Goldstein, Pioneer Lay Evangelist," *Church History* 52 (1983): 322-32.

14. Slawson, "Thirty Years of Street Preaching," p. 73.

15. Slawson, "Thirty Years of Street Preaching," p. 74.

preaching dramatically and intentionally embodies the public and political character of the basic Christian confession, "Jesus is Lord." As one participant in the anti-nuclear movement wrote,

> Whether at the gate of a bomber base, at a submarine station, or in front of a congressional office, being at a nuclear facility can provide Christians with the occasion to share the power and meaning of early apostolic faith. It is rather like the street preaching of the first century in downtown Rome. We can once again see that the routine proclamation of faith in Jesus, the simple theological affirmation of his lordship, is pregnant with political meaning.[16]

This kind of street witness has also taken the form of "liturgical direct action," through which believers bring Christian symbols and the "world-making power of liturgy" into the public arena.[17] In addition to confessing the sovereignty of God and exposing the idols of this age, street liturgies also publicly embody the vision of an alternative world. As Bill Wylie Kellermann has written of the public celebration of the Eucharist, "Gathered at the table, in the streets, the community sits down to a new social order."[18] In the process, the church engages in a public "war of myths," not against human enemies, but against the principalities and powers of the world.[19] The "collision" of which Kierkegaard speaks becomes acute in this form of street witness.

Solidarity

Every Wednesday morning, after serving breakfast to over one hundred homeless men, women, and children, volunteers at the Open Door Community go outside to worship with the homeless people

16. Mernie King, "Like Street Preaching in Downtown Rome: Witnessing at Nuclear Weapons Facilities," in *Waging Peace: A Handbook for the Struggle to Abolish Nuclear Weapons,* ed. Jim Wallis (San Francisco: Harper and Row, 1982), p. 210.

17. Bill Wylie Kellermann, *Seasons of Faith and Conscience: Kairos, Confession, Liturgy* (Maryknoll, New York: Orbis Books, 1991), p. 128.

18. Kellermann, *Seasons of Faith and Conscience,* p. 121.

19. Kellermann, *Seasons of Faith and Conscience,* p. 103. See Ephesians 6:12.

who gather in the community's front yard on Ponce de Leon Avenue, one of the busiest streets in the city. Knowing that homeless people are rarely welcomed into middle-class churches, the volunteers worship with them as an act of solidarity, much as George Whitefield went out to the poor when they were not welcomed in the Church of England. For their part, the homeless people embody the hospitality of Christian worship by welcoming the volunteers into their "living room." Standing in a circle and holding hands, the participants sing and pray, preach and testify amidst the noise of the rushing traffic. The goal is not to judge or convert. Rather, the two groups simply worship together as brothers and sisters in Christ, publicly embodying the diversity of the Christian community in the midst of a divided world. At a time when most churches discourage such worship, the streets provide the space where it can happen.

An Extreme Homiletic

As the preceding summary suggests, street preaching is a much broader and richer activity than contemporary stereotypes would suggest. Whatever form their preaching takes, however, street preachers have much to teach those of us who occupy pulpits on Sunday mornings. On the streets, superfluous layers are peeled away, and one is left with the very heart of preaching. Street preachers invite the rest of us back to the challenging and exhilarating essentials of our calling. They hold before us an "extreme homiletic."

On the streets, for example, all of the institutional trappings of preaching are stripped away. No pulpit offers security; no sanctuary provides a "safe space"; no ordination grants the preacher status and authority. Rather, preachers must rely on God's Word and the human voice alone. The words of John the Baptist, that paradigmatic preacher, take on new meaning: "I am the *voice* of one crying in the wilderness" (John 1:23). Word and voice. When everything else is stripped away, these two remain for preachers: absolute trust in the Word of God and faithful stewardship of the human voice.[20]

---

20. "Voice" here should not be interpreted too narrowly. "Voice," for example, may include "signing" for those who are deaf.

I read somewhere that preachers should roll up their Bibles and use them as megaphones when they proclaim the Word on the streets. For many of us, that may seem like a humorous and undignified image of the preacher. At root, however, that image captures the fundamental reality of preaching, which happens when the human voice is shaped and amplified by the Word of God. Word and voice. When these two come together, preaching happens. Street preachers remind us of the heart of our calling.

Moreover, by cutting through the trappings of organized religion, street preaching has historically challenged the exclusiveness of both the institutional church and the ordained ministry. The proclamation of the Word, street preachers have recognized, is the calling, not just of a select few, but of the entire church. On the streets women and lay people have been welcomed into the church's ministry of proclamation, even when they were not permitted into church pulpits. The streets have literally been a place where the voices of those oppressed by the church have been liberated to preach the Word. Whitefield and Wesley welcomed women and lay people into the preaching ministry. Catherine Booth and her daughter, Evangeline, themselves Salvation Army street preachers, created a space for women to proclaim the Word.[21] And even in the Roman Catholic Church, women and lay people were officially recognized as street preachers long before they were permitted to preach in the church.[22] On the streets, the Word has regularly burst its institutional bounds and created an inclusive ministry. Maybe that's why Melanie and other women in our classes have experienced the streets as such a liberating place to preach.

In addition, in a number of ways, street preachers remind the American church of the countercultural dimensions of the gospel. In a culture that seeks to relegate the Christian faith to the private sphere, street preachers embody the gospel's public claims. Street preachers remind us that the Word of God cannot be limited to the privacy of the

21. Donald W. Dayton and Lucille Sider Dayton, "Women as Preachers: Evangelical Precedents," *Christianity Today* (May 23, 1975): 4-7; Pamela J. Walker, "Proclaiming Women's Right to Preach," *Harvard Divinity Bulletin* 23, no. 3/4 (1994): 20-23, 35.

22. See Campbell, "A Catholic Salvation Army"; also Debra Campbell, "'I Can't Imagine Our Lady on an Outdoor Platform': Women in the Catholic Street Propaganda Movement," *U.S. Catholic Historian* 3 (1983): 103-14.

individual human heart or be contained within the walls of a pristine sanctuary. Rather, as Kierkegaard noted, the gospel belongs on the streets amidst the realities of public life. Whatever their particular message, street preachers enact this truth as they stand on street corners and proclaim the Word. They invite all of us who preach to take the gospel from the private sphere into the public arena. To do so constitutes a fundamental challenge to a culture that would privatize religion.

Such preaching also challenges a culture that has no room for fanatics. In a liberal culture, the one intolerable thing is fanaticism — unless, of course, one is a fanatical sports fan or a fanatical patriot. Street preachers, however, remind the rest of us that the gospel calls for a fanatical response, which involves the totality of our lives. Although this response too often takes a hateful and destructive (i.e., anti-Christian) form in many street preachers, nevertheless, the radical convictions of these preachers serve as a challenge to a church that all too often sells its soul in order to enjoy "freedom of religion."[23]

Finally, street preaching disrupts any notion that the gospel is a welcome Word in our culture. Preaching week in and week out among believers in the church, pulpit preachers can sometimes get lulled into a sense of complacency and forget that the gospel is often an alien Word in a strange land, a Word that people do not care to hear, a Word that creates conflict and resistance. After preaching on the streets one morning, Chris Michael, an experienced pastor, wrote of the "collision" between the gospel and the world — and of the excitement of preaching at the point of that "collision":

> Preaching on the street was the most elemental, basic, gut-wrenching preaching I have ever experienced. It was preaching in its purest form because it was the gospel confronting the world without the benefit of protection or comfort or order for the preacher. . . . On the street there is always the possibility that the spoken Word will cast out a demon or confront evil in such a way that open spiritual warfare will result. I felt that whenever anyone in our class preached it

23. On the temptations of American "freedom of religion," see Stanley Hauerwas, "The Politics of Freedom: Why Freedom of Religion Is a Subtle Temptation," in *After Christendom?* (Nashville: Abingdon Press, 1991), pp. 69-92.

was as if we were challenging the principalities and powers to reveal themselves for what they are. The sheer brazenness and audacity of challenging the world to hear a liberating gospel message . . . made street preaching the most exciting preaching I have done or experienced.

Street preaching offers a clear reminder that the gospel is a strange Word that the world does not always want to hear. It is the Word that led to Jesus' crucifixion. At the same time, however, street preaching challenges the church to recapture the audacity and exhilaration of speaking the odd Word of God before the powers of the world.[24]

24. A slightly different version of this essay by Chuck Campbell appeared as "The Word on the Streets" in the *Journal for Preachers* 22 (Pentecost 1999): 22-28.

Street Theater[1]

MATTHEW 21:1-11

In the past when I have read this well-known story from Matthew I have rushed immediately to Jesus' procession into Jerusalem — his "triumphal entry" as we have come to call it. As I studied the text this week, however, I noticed something new. Very little space is actually given to Jesus' entry into Jerusalem — only four verses are allotted to this event. Instead, most of the text — the first seven verses — deals with the *preparation* for the parade. And this fact tells us something important. The triumphal entry is not a spontaneous, spur-of-the-moment event. Rather, it is a carefully planned and thoroughly choreographed piece of street theater.[2] Jesus' "triumphal entry" is a drama that has been orchestrated down to the last detail.

Jesus begins at the Mount of Olives, which is no accident. Everyone knew the Mount of Olives was the place from which the final battle against Jerusalem's enemies would begin. From that location, the new king would inaugurate the liberation of Jerusalem. So Jesus

---

1. Chuck Campbell preached this sermon at the Open Door Community on Palm Sunday, 1996, several months before the 1996 Olympics in Atlanta. In their Palm Sunday service the community marks the beginning of their seven-day street vigil over Holy Week, during which time groups spend twenty-four-hour periods on the streets with homeless people.

2. The interpretation of Jesus' triumphal entry as "political street theater" comes from Ched Myers, *Binding the Strong Man: A Political Reading of Mark's Story of Jesus* (Maryknoll, New York: Orbis Books, 1988), pp. 294-96.

stands at the Mount of Olives, and we might hear a faint drum roll in the background as he prepares for this final campaign.

Then Jesus sends out for the provisions he will need for the battle — provisions for which he has made careful and elaborate arrangements in the city. But at this point things begin to get a little strange. Jesus does not send out for weapons or chariots or soldiers; he does not requisition B-52s or stealth bombers or cruise missiles. Instead, he directs his disciples to pick up a donkey and a colt. Jesus goes to take possession of Jerusalem unarmed and on a donkey!

Then the drama takes place, with many of the trappings of a military procession for a triumphant national hero — sort of like an ancient tickertape parade. And the people get all caught up in the event. They do the things a victorious military leader would expect. They spread palm leaves and cloaks before Jesus as a symbol of honor and acclaim. They shout, "Hosanna! Blessed is the one who comes in the name of the Lord." "God saves." "Long live the king!" And Jesus rides through the midst of the adoring crowds.

But the whole time, riding on his donkey (and in Matthew, at least, also on the colt!), Jesus is turning the world's notions of power and authority and rule on their head. Don't miss the humor in this drama. This "play" is a wonderful piece of political satire. We should probably imagine the event accompanied not by a drum roll and a precision marching band, but by a group of raucous New Orleans jazz musicians. In his "triumphal entry" Jesus lampoons all the powers of the world with their pretensions to glory and dominion.

And we know those powers; we've heard their voices:

"Mine is the kingdom," say the nations, as they strut around like peacocks, demanding our absolute loyalty.

"Mine is the power," says the Pentagon, as it promises us salvation through a new generation of high-tech weapons.

"Mine is the glory," says old mammon, as he hoards his gold and crushes the poor beneath his feet.

"Amen and Amen!" all too often shouts the church, giving its blessing to the ways of the world.

We know these powers. We've heard their voices, and we've seen the havoc they can wreak. Well, riding into Jerusalem on his donkey,

Jesus unmasks their pretensions to power and glory. And Jesus enacts an alternative.

> He comes not as one who lords his authority over others, but as one who rejects domination and comes as a servant;
> He comes not as a mighty warrior, but as one who refuses to rely on violence;
> He comes not with pomp and wealth, but as one identified with the poor.

Jesus performs the words of the prophet Zechariah (9:9). He takes those old, old words and turns them into a living drama:

> Tell the daughter of Zion,
> Look, your king is coming to you,
> > humble and mounted on a donkey,
> > and on a colt, the foal of a donkey.
>
> (Matthew 21:5)

Jesus fulfills the words of the prophet and enacts the subversive reign of God in the midst of the city. This theater, Matthew proclaims, is God's theater. This drama is God's drama. This way is God's way. Here is the story that really matters; here is the story that endures.

And the city realizes something is up. The whole place is in turmoil, shaken at its very foundations, as if struck by an earthquake. All the self-sufficiency and wealth and power on which the city has been built begin to quake in the face of Jesus' little drama.

In this street theater, Jesus makes the gospel public and political. He claims the city — its economics, its politics, its culture — for the way of God. And Jerusalem is shaken. And that kind of claim will set our society in turmoil as well. For our society wants to keep the Christian faith private. That's the way "freedom of religion" operates. You're free to believe what you want — in the privacy of your own heart and home and church. But don't bring the claims of Jesus into the public arena. There we operate by other standards.

And the same thing is true of Atlanta, particularly in this Olympic year. The Olympic Committee doesn't want a public Jesus, who lampoons all the pomp and ceremony as he enters the city humbly, riding on a donkey. The business community doesn't want a public Jesus, who comes into the city identified with the poor. And the City Council certainly doesn't want a public Jesus who comes to claim their thrones. "You're welcome to your faith — in private. But your little pieties can't be taken seriously in the public arena." These powers, however, don't understand the entry into Jerusalem. For in his triumphal entry, Jesus claims the city in a most public and political way.

And the church itself often doesn't understand this story either. We too have often opted for a private, nonthreatening Christianity. We have all too often been satisfied helping individuals cope with the way things are, rather than seeking to form a disciplined people able to stand against the pretensions and illusions of the world. And as a consequence, the church causes little turmoil in the city.

In his "Letter from Birmingham City Jail," Martin Luther King, Jr., captured the reality of the contemporary church all too well:

> Wherever the early Christians entered a town the power structure got disturbed and immediately sought to convict them for being "disturbers of the peace" and "outside agitators." But they went on with the conviction that they were "a colony of heaven," and had to obey God rather than [human beings]. . . .
>
> Things are different now. The contemporary church is often a weak, ineffectual voice with an uncertain sound. It is so often the arch-supporter of the status quo. Far from being disturbed by the presence of the church, the power structure of the average community is consoled by the church's silent and often vocal sanction of things as they are.[3]

Like a jagged rock thrown into a flowing stream, the church once "troubled the waters." Now, however, it seems as if the church has slowly, often imperceptibly been worn so smooth by the culture that it no longer creates any disturbance at all.

But each year on Palm Sunday, Jesus' street theater, his performance of the old words of the prophet, calls us back to the public char-

---

3. Martin Luther King, Jr., "Letter from Birmingham City Jail," in *A Testament of Hope: The Essential Writings of Martin Luther King, Jr.,* ed. James Melvin Washington (San Francisco: Harper and Row, 1986), p. 300.

acter of the gospel — to the troubling, alternative politics of God. Jesus invites us to follow him into the city and claim it for the purposes of God. Jesus invites us to become participants in his street theater.

And, God knows, Atlanta needs Jesus' street theater right now. Atlanta needs to be reminded of the drama that really matters and the story that endures. For Atlanta has become a rather crazy place while preparing for the Olympics. The city has become much like a person Walter Brueggemann remembers from an event during his childhood.

When Brueggemann was in the sixth grade a twin-engine plane crashed in a cornfield near his home. With his friends, Brueggemann ran to watch as the ambulance crew, with rubber gloves, pulled pieces of human beings out of the wreckage and put them in plastic bags. The memory that lingers most vividly, Brueggemann recalls, is that of "watching a woman standing next to me holding a baby, eating an apple." Brueggemann remembers wondering, "How can she do that, now, here?" Later in his life, as he reflected on those childhood feelings, Brueggemann came to understand his bewilderment. "She had no shame," he concludes. "She had no sense of incongruity, no sense of disproportion." The woman, like many Americans, had somehow lost the capacity to blush at the absurdity and obscenity of her actions.[4]

That's the way I feel about Atlanta right now. We have lost our sense of incongruity and disproportion. We have lost our ability to blush at the absurdities all around us:

> Like spending millions of dollars on a two-week extravaganza for the wealthy while thousands of people in this city remain homeless and hungry.
> Like building ritzy new Olympic housing right down the street from a public housing project where kids play in areas poisoned with lead.
> Like using the labor of homeless men to construct Olympic venues, then sweeping those men off the streets because they are bad for the city's image.

---

4. Brueggemann's story is recounted in P. C. Ennis, Jr., "The Things That Make for Peace," *Journal for Preachers* 6, no. 5 (1983): 19.

All of this, and more, is going on right before our eyes, but "the powers that be" stand around eating apples, slapping each other on the back, oblivious to the obscenity of it all.

And that's why it's important for this community to take the drama of Palm Sunday and Holy Week to the streets of the city this year. Through our "street theater" we bear witness to the incongruities and the obscenities, and we claim the city for the purposes of God. Tonight a group will process into the heart of the city and spend the night on the streets. Every other day and night this week different groups will follow the steps of homeless people along the way of the cross. And each afternoon, this community will worship in public places that have an impact on the lives of the poor. Through this street theater, we will bear witness to that odd ruler who comes into the city humble and riding on a donkey. And we will seek to unmask the pretensions of power and wealth and self-sufficiency that drive the city.

Now, our little gospel theater certainly won't compare to the grand theater of the Olympics, for which the sets are rising all around us. Our little groups probably won't cause the city to shake as if an earthquake had hit. Indeed, we may not even create a small tremor. But that's okay. We are not the Savior — and we don't have to be. Jesus is the Savior. And Jesus has already entered the city and shaken its foundations. We just have to join Jesus there. We just have to go remind the city of what Jesus has already done and continues to do.

And because we simply join Jesus in *his* drama, we can enter the city with humility and hope and humor — even in the shadow of the cross. We might even take a New Orleans jazz band with us. For we know that the drama of Holy Week is the one that really matters; it is the story that endures. And we know that we are in the right struggle.

So come now to the table. Come take your places in the drama. Come eat and drink the meal that will sustain you through the week.

SOLIDARITY

*Commit yourselves to the same practical reasoning that you see
and have in Christ Jesus,*

> *who, though he was fully God,*
> *did not use his equality with God for his own advantage,*
> *but gave up everything,*
> *becoming a slave in every way,*
> *having been born just like any other human.*
> *And when he had become like one of us,*
> *he placed himself in solidarity with the humiliated,*
> *following the way of obedience to the point of death*
> *— even death on a cross.*

PHILIPPIANS 2:5-8

Blessed Are the Poor in Spirit

Relief print from sintra plate; 14 ½″ × 12″; © 1997 Christina Bray

"You Have Made Them Equal to Us": Human Solidarity in the Household of God

MATTHEW 20:12

Every morning in Atlanta, before most of us get out of bed, thousands of desperately poor women and men get up, leave behind whatever shelter they have, and go in search of work. Many of the men end up in lines at one of Atlanta's "labor pools," where they will compete for back-breaking, often demeaning jobs at the minimum wage. They will typically lose a substantial portion even of that paltry sum because their employers will charge them for transportation, hats, and gloves. They are often hungry throughout the day. At the Butler Street Breakfast we have often seen men leave behind full bowls of hot grits because the call for work came and there was no time to eat. The fact that these men are "temporary people" also means that they receive no benefits of any kind. They are "lucky" to receive as much as twenty-five dollars at the end of the day, not enough to supply a single individual in this economy with adequate housing and food, let alone to support a family.

The plight of the poor in places like Atlanta is not a new story, but one that has been repeated over and over again throughout history. Perhaps the endless repetition of this scenario has made many of us callous, even blind to these realities. According to the Bible, callousness, blindness, and numbness are all symptoms of the condition of humans who have turned their backs on God (cf., e.g., Ephesians 4:17-24). They are the other side of the coin of the sins against our sisters

117

and brothers that we call poverty, the loss of dignity, and homelessness. Together, these are the (in)human symptoms of our unwillingness to live in solidarity with one another and to live by faith in a God who promises to give us what we need today.

Matthew's Gospel includes a story that describes circumstances remarkably similar to those of the poor in cities like Atlanta, implicitly relating these circumstances to the absence of human solidarity. The "Parable of the Workers of the Vineyard" (Matthew 20:1-16) is not just a lifelike rendition of the economic realities of the ancient (and modern) world, but a warning to the callous. But more than just negative criticism, it offers us a vision of what the reign of God is like, and points us toward the kinds of relationships required in the "household" that calls on this merciful God as "patron" and "benefactor."

In this parable, Jesus tells of a "householder," i.e., a landowner, who goes out early in the morning to hire laborers for his vineyard. He agrees to pay these workers about a denarius a day, roughly the equivalent of a "minimum wage" in the economy of Jesus' day (but unlike our "minimum wage," a denarius may actually have been enough to live on). Later in the morning he goes again to the marketplace and hires still more laborers, but he tells them only that he will pay them "what is right." Twice more, at the sixth and ninth hours, he goes again to the marketplace and hires still more workers. Finally, at about the eleventh hour, about an hour before the end of daylight, he hires the last group of workers that he finds standing idle in the marketplace.

As in most of Jesus' parables, the story he tells is rooted in everyday experience. In particular, Jesus is describing the experience of the poor of his day. In the ancient economy there was no middle class to speak of, and the vast majority of the population lived in varying degrees of "poverty." But the situation of the day laborer was particularly critical, usually even worse than that of a slave. Slaves, at least, had the advantage of being considered someone's property, and thus as a resource to be used for the benefit of the household (which included not only kin but a variety of people who had financial or social obligations to the householder). Day laborers, however, did not have ongoing attachments to any household and were considered less than human. As a consequence, they lived on the edge of survival, without adequate shelter or food. As expendable people without rights or access to the courts, they were always at a disadvantage in their dealings with those who hired them, and were often exploited. Their life expectancy would have fallen short of even that of most ancient people (around thirty-two to thirty-three years!). Five or six years was the best one could typically expect once one fell to the class of day laborer.

Like the urban poor of Atlanta, day laborers were held in general contempt by the rest of the population, even by those whose social and economic location was just a step above. Then as now, there was a widespread tendency to "blame the victims" of the economy for their plight. Because the ancient Mediterranean economy was structured around patronage, it was typical for people to spend whatever income they generated on gifts for those with whom they sought to curry favor. As a consequence, there was no incentive to give to those from whom you could expect nothing in return. Charity, in other words, was not a widely exercised or highly honored practice.

This background may help us understand one of the more striking elements of the parable, namely, the fact that this particular householder goes repeatedly to the marketplace throughout the day to hire more laborers. While some scholars have speculated that he was repeatedly surprised by the size of the harvest and thus required more workers, the story itself suggests that he was concerned that there would not be anyone idle (cf. 20:3, 6). In other words, for some reason this householder is not so much concerned about the personal costs of all his hiring, nor about the size of the harvest, but rather about the necessity to find work for those who are at loss in the economy. He is not even content to send his steward to do this hiring, which would have been typical of wealthy landowners, but goes himself and engages them firsthand.

This little surprise is typical of Jesus' parables, which usually begin with descriptions of everyday events and experience but then introduce some incongruity, an action or saying that causes the listener to rethink his or her presuppositions about the world. Parables were Jesus' favorite way of teaching about the "reign of heaven," a reality that he could not adequately describe in terms of the everyday experience of a broken world. He had to explode his hearers' imaginations, so that it became possible for them to discern the world-jarring character of God's presence and power. Thus Jesus' parables, especially the parables about the "reign of God" (cf. 20:1), work with conventional experience only to move beyond it to what seems strange and even threatening — all in order to point toward the astonishing realities of God.

If the householder's persistent attempts to find work for expendable day laborers would have been cause for surprise among the ancient audience of this parable, his payment strategies would have seemed still more strange. He issues payment in reverse of the hiring order, so that those who were hired at the end of the day are paid first. Even more surprising, they receive a full denarius — the same wage as the householder had arranged with those who began work at the start of the day. With some reason, then, those who were hired at the start of the day approach the time of payment with the expectation that they will receive even more than the denarius to which they had agreed. Not so. Not only does this householder hire everyone he can throughout the day, he also pays them the same wage regardless of how long they worked. This is apparently what he means when he tells the workers hired throughout the day that he will pay them "what is right" (20:4).

In the face of these circumstances, many of us would probably sympathize with the resentment of the day-long workers: "These last worked only one hour, and you have made them equal to us who have borne the burden of the day and the scorching heat" (20:12). Apparently they do not share the householder's sense of "what is right." They would probably prefer to preserve a sense of "justice" rooted in merit, rather than in the "goodness" of the householder. When he hears their complaints, the householder reminds these workers both of the terms of the original contract and of his authority to dispense his property as he sees fit (20:14-15). His explanation is only partly satisfying, however, for what most of us find offensive is not the householder's exercise of executive rights over his property, but the effects his actions have in terms of leveling the economic playing field. This accounts in large part for the difficulty many of us have in "making sense" of this parable. Is this the way God really is? Is this really the way God intends to treat us?

While most of us from time to time express dismay at the exorbitant incomes public figures, athletes, executives, and some others command in our economy, we all nonetheless accept as normal — even good — the disparate levels of pay workers in our economy receive for different kinds of work. Part of the reason we accept this reality as normal and good is that we use these disparities to mark distinctions of class and status, as well as race and gender, among us. Thus, like the laborers hired at the beginning of the day, we think we deserve what we get and more. Like them we might accept attempts to find work for everyone in the marketplace, but we would deeply resent payment plans that "make us all equal." Imagine a world in which a doctor, a lawyer, or a professor receives the same pay as a McDonald's employee, a garbage collector, or a cleaning woman — just a living wage for the day. Unthinkable! (It's worth noting, however, that in Jesus' day, doctors, lawyers, and professors were often classified as slaves!) We would rather preserve some sense of difference, some privilege, so that we can tell ourselves that we are more secure, more blessed, more righteous than others around us.

The purpose of this parable, however, is probably not just to criticize the day-long workers and those among us who sympathize with them, but to teach us about the necessity of solidarity in the household of God. The parable of the workers of the vineyard is just one of many stories and teachings in this section of Matthew that depict how humans ought to respond to the reign of a merciful God who promises to give us what we need today (cf. Matthew 6:25-34). Among those who share this conviction about God there is no reason to fail in mercy, but every reason to forgive (18:23-35). There is no reason to hoard what we have, but every reason to share what we have with the poor (19:16-30). There is no reason to jockey for position, or to lord it over one another, but every reason to serve one another (20:20-28). In all of these episodes Jesus is pointing us away from the practices that we have come to understand as "normal" and "natural" in our human household and towards the radical practices that make it possible for us to live in God's presence.

Christians have always affirmed that God is merciful, a conviction that is especially dear to Matthew. Most of the time we think of this mercy in personal terms, as God overlooking this or that sin, or rescuing us from this or that crisis. Jesus has different notions. He wants us to understand that to affirm the reality of a merciful God is to challenge the way we relate to the "least ones" (25:31-46), the children, and the "expendables." He knows that we will never fully comprehend God's mercy until we learn to live in solidarity with the day laborers of our own world. And for those of us who think we have

121

earned God's special blessings, and who resent the possibility of equality with those who've come late to the vineyard, the risk of overlooking God's mercy is particularly acute.

What might this mean for us more concretely? It means that our "salvation," our experience and discernment of God's mercy, is directly, inextricably, absolutely, and thoroughly tied to the relationships we have with our fellow humans, especially those people we tend to discount. We will discern God's mercy most clearly when we take the steps necessary to put ourselves in relationship with such people. There is no formula for this; we just need to do whatever it takes to get close to them — close enough to listen, to learn with them, and to share their sorrows and joys, their vulnerability and their anger, as well as their faith. In most cases this will require us to leave behind our homes, our securities, our schedules, and our stereotypes. The next steps follow gracefully from these first steps, though they will sometimes be shadowed by confusion and doubt. And how will we know that we are on the right path? We will know we are on the path of solidarity and discipleship when the words "You have made them equal to us" roll off our lips not in bitterness and resentment, but in grateful praise of the merciful God of Jesus Christ.[1]

---

1. This sermon was preached by Stan Saunders at the Open Door in February of 1997. It later appeared in *Hospitality* 16 (April 1997): 1-2.

Scapegoating the Homeless

On Wednesday, October 2nd, 1996, at 11:52 P.M. I was placed under arrest, along with Ed Loring and Ron Jackson from the Open Door and seven students from Columbia Seminary. Our crime: sitting and talking in Woodruff Park after 11:00 P.M. (at tables and chairs provided for such conversation).

As part of a seminary course entitled "good news to the poor," our group was spending twenty-four hours on the streets with our homeless brothers and sisters. Our evening began at 5:00 P.M., and by 10:30 we were at Woodruff Park with many experiences to share and discuss. At 10:40 a police officer announced that the park would close in twenty minutes. We returned to our conversation and remained in the park past closing time. At 11:52 we were told we had broken a city ordinance by staying in the park after 11:00, and we were placed under arrest without any further warning. We offered to leave the park immediately, which should have accomplished the purpose of the ordinance — keeping the park empty overnight. We were told, however, that we *had* to be arrested. That was the new policy regarding after-hours visitors to the park: immediate arrest. "If we're going to arrest *them*," one officer said, pointing to several homeless people, "we have to arrest you as well."

We pleaded our case to no avail as the officer took down our names and addresses. Finally, upon our request, a supervisor was called and arrived on the scene. After a brief discussion, she discharged us, and we left the park. Our white, middle-class privilege had come to our aid and gotten us released. But we felt okay because the police said they would not arrest anyone else in the park that night. (There was no one remaining to arrest anyway because everyone else had left the park while the police were dealing with us.) Homeless people were thus spared a sweep for at least one night. And our group was able to continue with our plans. Everything turned out okay on October 2nd.

But everything is not okay in downtown Atlanta. As we later discovered, October 2nd marked the beginning of a concerted effort by city officials and business leaders to run homeless people out of downtown using legal means. Not only has the crackdown continued in Woodruff Park, but new city ordinances have been passed making many activities of homeless people a crime, including nonaggressive panhandling and "urban camping" (a rather chic euphemism for lying down to rest in a public place when you have nowhere else to sleep). The function of these ordinances, as I discovered in the park, is *not* to prevent crime, but rather to *create criminals*. Just as the police used a city ordinance to make criminals out of our group in Woodruff Park, so the new ordinances make criminals of many homeless people who are simply trying to survive on the streets. Homelessness is becoming a crime in Atlanta (and in many other cities around the country), and jail is becoming the public housing of first resort — a dramatic shift from the days when people viewed the homeless sympathetically and sought to bring an end to this social evil through constructive means.

What is going on downtown? This "solution" to the problem of homelessness is so shortsighted and inadequate, so bizarre and inhuman, how can people support it? What is at the root of our need to turn homeless people into criminals? I have thought about these questions often since that night in the park. No doubt, the answers to them involves complex social, psychological, political, and economic factors.

Without discounting these factors, however, I have come to believe that a profound and troubling *theological* reality lies at the root of these ordinances: Atlanta, in the name of its powerful, privileged citizens, has begun to engage in the ancient ritual of scapegoating. Such a ritual has become necessary because those of us who are privileged simply are not willing to confront honestly the evil of homelessness. If we did, we would have to face the sins of capitalism as well as the incongruities in our own lifestyles. We would have to confront, as William Stringfellow puts it, the radical fallenness of America as well as our own active and passive roles in perpetuating evil. We would have to relinquish the illusion of our own righteousness and turn to confession and repentance. And that is just too much to bear for most Americans, who consider ourselves to be "good people."

So the solution is scapegoating — transferring the guilt from ourselves to the most vulnerable people in our society and punishing them accordingly. If blame can be shifted from the society and the privileged to the homeless, then we upper-class and middle-class folks can once again feel good about ourselves, having exorcised our guilt by transferring it to someone else. Making criminals out of homeless people, it turns out, is a perfect way to accomplish this goal — a perfect means of scapegoating. If the activities of those who are homeless can be made into crimes, then they can be "justly" condemned, and the rest of us are off the hook. If homeless people can be turned into criminals, then the sin and guilt of our social order can be heaped upon their shoulders. The rest of us can breathe easy, absolved of our own sin and guilt as we drive the homeless from our midst (into jail), just as Israel sent a sin-laden goat into the wilderness on the Day of Atonement (Leviticus 16:20-22). Unlike in Israel, however, in Atlanta there is no confession of sin by the people and no recognition of what we are doing. Rather, homeless people have become the scapegoat by means of which the rest of us seek to reassure ourselves of our own righteousness and our society's goodness.

In Atlanta and other cities across the nation the ancient ritual of scapegoating is being enacted once again in ordinances designed not to prevent crime, but to create criminals. As Christians, therefore, we oppose these ordinances not simply for practical, political, or economic reasons. Rather, we oppose the ordinances for theological reasons. We know that the ultimate victim of scapegoating is the crucified Jesus, who stands in solidarity with all of society's scapegoats and challenges this entire social ritual at its roots. And we know that in Jesus Christ we have the resources of confession and repentance, imagination and hope, which enable us to say "No!" to scapegoating and which free us to live out a different vision of God's city.[1]

1. This essay by Chuck Campbell originally appeared in *Hospitality* 16 (February 1997): 4.

A Song of Solidarity
with the Humiliated[1]

2:1 *Your life in Christ makes you strong, and Christ's love comforts you. You have fellowship in the Spirit, and kindness and compassion for one another.* 2*But if this is so, then make my joy complete by focusing on the same thing, having the same love, being in full accord and of one mind.* 3*Don't do what you do because of jealousy or selfish ambition or conceit, but humbly regard others as better than yourselves.* 4*Pay attention to one another's interests, not just your own.* 5*Commit yourselves to the same practical reasoning that you see and have in Christ Jesus,*

> 6*who, though he was fully God,*
> *did not use his equality with God for his own advantage,*
> 7*but gave up everything,*
> *becoming a slave in every way,*
> *having been born just like any other human.*
> *And when he had become like one of us,*
> 8*he placed himself in solidarity with the humiliated,*
> *following the way of obedience to the point of death*
> *— even death on a cross.*

1. This sermon was preached by Stan Saunders at the Open Door Community on Palm Sunday, 1999. In this service of worship the community marks the beginning of its seven-day street vigil during Holy Week.

126

A Song of Solidarity with the Humiliated

⁹For this reason God gave Christ the highest place
and gave him the one name that is above every name,
¹⁰so that at the name of Jesus everyone will bow down,
in heaven and on earth and under the earth,
¹¹and all will openly affirm that Jesus Christ is Lord,
to the glory of God the Father.

PHILIPPIANS 2:1-11[2]

This is Holy Week, the time when people in churches all over the world recall the suffering, death, and resurrection of Christ. It's also the time of year, along with the Festival of Shelters in the Fall, when the members of the Open Door participate in a form of spiritual discipline that is peculiar to this community. By "spiritual discipline" I mean disciplined action in the Spirit of Christ — in this case in the form of twenty-four-hour street vigils with the homeless people of Atlanta. I suspect that there are many folks, even in the churches and perhaps among the homeless themselves, who might regard this exercise as foolish, or not worth the risks, or as merely a token gesture. On the basis of the passage we have just read from Paul's letter to the Philippians, I would want to argue rather that it is a foundational form of witness, not just about who and what this community is, but more importantly, a witness to who God is. In fact, I want to claim that according to Paul's standards anything short of this kind of embodied witness to the weakness of the cross falls short of his definition of what it means to be Christian.

Before we go very far in this passage I need to warn you about it. There is good historical reason to conclude that immersion into this passage has the potential to shape our imagination and practices in decisive ways. One person who loved this passage and conformed her life to its notes was Dorothy Day, one of the founders of the Catholic Worker Movement and, of course, a person whose life and writings have in turn profoundly shaped the life of this community. Ernst Lohmeyer, a German New Testament professor, studied this passage in detail and first determined that it was a hymn. In the 1920s

2. Author's translation.

Lohmeyer was a professor at Breslau, a fairly prestigious appointment, but was removed from this position because he was an opponent of the Nazis. He managed to obtain a teaching position in what was to become East Germany. In 1945 he was appointed Rector of the University at Greifswald, but was arrested before he could assume this position. In 1946 Lohmeyer was executed by the Communists. He followed both Jesus and Paul in being a victim of what some have called "judicial murder."[3] Both of these people were genuine Christian witnesses, people who testify with their lives that the God of the world is none other than Jesus of Nazareth who died on a cross. The real Christians in this world are people whose lives conform to this hymn.

Now about the passage itself. It's called the Christ Hymn, and it's one of the foundational pieces of christological confession found in the New Testament. With this hymn we are very close to the beginnings of early Christianity. I suspect that this is one of the hymns the first Christians chanted or sang together at their eucharistic meals. In any case, Paul cites it here in a way that suggests he thought the Christians in Philippi would know it well.

How might the Christians in Philippi have understood this hymn? What did their "confession" of Jesus as the humble yet exalted Christ mean in their world? It may help to recall that Philippi was a Roman colony, a city where the soldiers of the conquering Roman army had taken over the land and served now as the leading citizens. It was a place full of the trappings of the Roman Empire, where military presence and activities were common. Some scholars have recently argued that Philippi may have been the place where Paul himself was eventually executed, which would lend poignancy to his musings about his own death earlier in the letter (Philippians 1:20-26).[4] In any case, we know from the letter that Paul is a prisoner, probably in Ephesus, at the time he writes this letter. Imagine a prisoner, one who faces the possibility of being executed

3. Lohmeyer's book on the Christ Hymn in Philippians 2, *Kyrios Jesus,* was first published in 1928. Some of his story is recounted in Colin Brown, "Ernst Lohmeyer's *Kyrios Jesus,*" in *Where Christology Began: Essays on Philippians 2,* ed. Ralph P. Martin and Brian J. Dodd (Louisville: Westminster/John Knox Press, 1998), pp. 6-42, especially p. 41n4.

4. See the essays in Charalambos Bakirtzis and Helmut Koester, eds., *Philippi at the Time of Paul and after His Death* (Harrisburg, Pennsylvania: Trinity Press International, 1998).

by the Roman state, writing these words. Paul is not merely discussing religious matters in this letter, nor even matters of "doctrine." He's talking about life and death, Jesus' death and his own. And he's holding these up for everyone to see. He's saying that this kind of life is what the God of the universe honors.

The primary problem Paul seems to be dealing with in the Philippian congregation is one that has beset churches throughout Christian history, namely, Christians pursuing their own self-interests and self-aggrandizement in the name of Christ, with factions as the result. Some in the congregation even question Paul's authority, perhaps because he keeps having conflicts with the authorities and because he seems less honorable than they might like a leader to be. At the beginning of this letter, Paul self-consciously identifies himself as a slave of Jesus Christ, as if to emphasize the fact of his dishonorable circumstances, brought about by his conformity to the image of Jesus. In the third chapter he runs his résumé out for everyone to see — and it's a good one — only to say that he really doesn't think it's worth much in comparison to knowing Christ crucified (3:4-11). When we think about Paul reciting this hymn for the Philippian Christians, we need to remind ourselves that he is here a self-proclaimed prisoner and slave, not one of the mighty theologians or preachers we like to honor in the church today. The Christ Hymn, in other words, is a song for prisoners and slaves. It's a song for the people at the Open Door, and for the people who live in the yard and on the streets and in our jails.

Paul presents the hymn as a form of practical, communal wisdom, centered on and made possible in Jesus Christ (2:5).[5] In other words, he wants the Christians in Philippi to live and breathe this hymn to the point that it becomes the most elemental stuff in their individual and communal consciousness, the lens through which they look at the world. The hymn itself falls into two parts, verses 6-8, which tell the story of Jesus' incarnation, life, and crucifixion, and verses 9-11, which recount his exaltation. The two parts of the hymn need to be read together as a kind of paradox. Some Christians con-

---

5. The language of "practical wisdom" or "practical reasoning" is borrowed from Wayne A. Meeks, "The Man from Heaven in Paul's Letter to the Philippians," in *The Future of Early Christianity: Essays in Honor of Helmut Koester,* ed. Birger Pearson (Minneapolis: Fortress Press, 1991), pp. 329-36.

sider the crucifixion a terrible mistake, one that God erases when Jesus is raised from the dead. But for Paul, the exaltation of Jesus does not wipe out the crucifixion; rather it confirms it. It says, "This way — the way of self-emptying, solidarity with the humiliated, and crucifixion — this way of life is what God affirms and exalts."

As the early Christians heard the story of Jesus in these verses, they would also have heard language that resonated deeply with Isaiah's vision of the suffering servant (i.e., Israel), found in the poetry of Isaiah. This is important because it suggests that the hymn was and is not only about Jesus, but about all of God's people. Even the second stanza, announcing the exaltation of the crucified Jesus, tells part of our story. The language of verses 10-11, for example, is borrowed from Isaiah 45, which recounts the last days vision of God's vindication of suffering Israel and the gathering of the nations to worship God. But Isaiah 45:23 says that at *God's* name every knee will bow and every tongue confess. In the hymn, Jesus' name replaces the name of God. In other words, Jesus is given "the name," not just the name Jesus, but the "holy name." And this naming is associated in Isaiah's vision (and Paul's) with the gathering of the nations to worship Israel's God. That's why Paul pursues his mission among the Gentiles. And that, in turn, is why the Philippian congregation even exists, and why we are here today. In other words, the telling of this story is what brings the beloved community, the new community of the last days, into being. So, this hymn is not only Jesus' story, but our story, too.

But most of all, it's the story of God. Without question this hymn affirms the denial of self-interest, as well as the divestment of human status and privilege. It even seems to suggest that Jesus gives up his divinity. But this is not so. Jesus does not give up his divine identity so much as he expresses it perfectly by becoming a slave. This is an important nuance. It means that by becoming human, a slave, and crucified, Jesus demonstrates for us who God really is. And this in turn reminds us of where we should look for God when we go out onto the streets this week.

But if Jesus does not give up his divine nature, he surely does relinquish his claims upon the status and privilege of divinity. He also manifests true humility, a word that we usually understand as a form of personal virtue, akin to meekness and modesty. These are perfectly good virtues, but what this word really signifies is solidarity with the humiliated, the complete identification of oneself with those who are at the very bottom of the human refuse pile. Solidarity with the humiliated is not the same as solidarity with the humble. Lots of us consider ourselves humble — we may even be proud of our humility. But we aren't the humiliated of this world. We only have to go to the front door of this building and into the yard where our homeless friends live to see the difference. When Jesus comes into this world and becomes a slave, he is not merely modeling the importance of being a humble guy. He is not practicing patronizing condescension. He is embodying solidarity with the humiliated.[6] Jesus' kind of "humility" fundamentally undermines worldly norms and perceptions of power. When we understand what this hymn means by humility and what it tells us about who God is, we have to agree with the Bolivian farm worker who said, "An atheist is someone who fails to practice justice towards the poor."[7]

For Paul, for the Philippians, and for us, this hymn brings into focus the drama of salvation, which here is the story of God entering the world in solidarity with the least ones. For Paul, then, salvation is not a matter of never sinning, or never touching those we consider unclean, or being rescued from this world. It's not a matter of having our sins taken away and joining the ranks of a comfortable middle-class congregation. Salvation is rather the obedience to God that is embodied in the active practice of solidarity with the humiliated.

This hymn of, by, and for slaves and prisoners reminds the choir of the foundational notes and tones of its existence: the intentional divestment of advantage, and solidarity with the humiliated in the name of Jesus Christ, and all so that the God we know in Jesus Christ crucified might be glorified. When we go out this week onto the streets, to walk with the humiliated, to eat with them and sleep where they sleep, it might be useful to sing with Paul this audacious song of the slaves and prisoners, a song about the God who is a slave and a slave who is God. When we do so, we join ourselves with Paul and the Philippians, we offer more perfect praise to God, and we participate in bringing God's church into being.

---

6. Klaus Wengst, *Humility: Solidarity with the Humiliated*, trans. John Bowden (Philadelphia: Fortress Press, 1988).

7. Quoted by Gustavo Gutiérrez, *The Power of the Poor in History* (Maryknoll, New York: Orbis Books, 1983), p. 140, cited in Wengst, *Humility*, p. 60.

Again . . . and Again . . . and Again

During my volunteer work at the Open Door, one thing happened that I never would have expected in my wildest imagination. I met Sye Pressley, a jazz saxophonist living at 910, and he began to teach me music theory. The process was not always a pleasant one. I would bump into Sye at 6:00 in the morning before the Butler Street Breakfast, and he would start firing questions: "What is a cycle of fifths?" "How many tones are in a scale?" "How many flats are in the A-flat major scale?" All of this was tacit knowledge for Sye — knowledge he didn't even have to think about; it was "in his bones." My head, however, would spin as I struggled to recall the scales and counted fourths and fifths on my fingers. At each mistake, Sye would correct me: "Do it again. You'll never be a jazz musician until all of this is second nature. Do it again . . . and again . . . and again." I had become an apprentice to a mentor, who was trying to train me in the skills of the jazz musician.

This model, I have come to realize, has also shaped my education with the Open Door and Urban Training Organization. Whether "on the streets" with Ed Loring, at the prison with Murphy Davis, in the housing projects with Dewey Merritt (of UTOA), or at the Infectious Disease Clinic with "Famous Amos" Jones (a former resident at the Open Door, who had AIDS), I have been an apprentice to various mentors. Skills that are second nature to them, I have had to begin learning through continual trial and error, often through seemingly insignificant actions. (During the Festival of Shelters, for example, when I was supposed to embody solidarity with the homeless, I walked into City

132

Hall and bought myself a soft drink for lunch. ("Think about what you did, Chuck," I was told. "Try it again . . . and again . . . and again.") In order to enter even slightly into the world of the poor, I have had to undertake the discipline of an apprentice, recognizing my limitations, giving up control, following my mentors' lead. I have had to become a learner in what Susan Thistlethwaite calls a "grassroots mentoring program":

> The learner in a grassroots mentoring program enters slowly into a different culture and learns to respect its differences. The one who is mentored does not expect that he or she will immediately be given trust and responsibility. Larger systems of social and economic exploitation make a quick jump to trust impossible. Through learning to cross boundaries and cooperate with others without exploitation, the learner gradually is apprenticed in the ability to see from different points of view and to act in genuine solidarity with those who are marginalized in our society.[1]

The most difficult part has been giving up control. As a white, well-educated, middle-class male, I am accustomed to being in control. When a situation feels chaotic, I'm immediately ready to impose an order of my own making. When something seems broken, my immediate response is to fix it with my own solution. This is how people in positions of dominance and power deal with things. And I have noticed that this is the way many white, middle-class people deal with poor people. With the best of intentions we often immediately try to impose our own order on their lives, to "rehabilitate" them according to our values, to force our solutions on their problems — all before we have taken the time to enter into their world and value them as "other," all before we have begun to stand in genuine solidarity with them. The most visible recent consequence of this approach is a welfare-reform program based on the threat, "Get to work or else!"

All of my mentors, I came to realize, have been trying to train me

---

1. Susan B. Thistlethwaite, "Beyond Theological Tourism," in *Beyond Theological Tourism: Mentoring as a Grassroots Approach to Theological Education,* ed. Susan B. Thistlethwaite and George F. Cairns (Maryknoll, New York: Orbis Books, 1994), p. 15.

not in the middle-class skills of problem-solving (indeed, I had to unlearn some of these), but in the more fundamental skills of solidarity with those who are marginalized. As I continue to be reminded almost daily, these skills are acquired very slowly — and often painfully — and they are easily lost if not regularly practiced. A person like myself, who has much to learn and much to lose, cannot expect to develop or retain these skills in any less time or with any less effort than it takes to become a jazz saxophonist. The refrain never ends: Again . . . and again . . . and again.

For many of us, this process involves dying — dying to personal identities based on position and privilege and control, dying to old, comfortable ways of being in the world. But this process of dying is in fact a way of living into our baptisms, for along this path lies the promise of new life. Jesus put it this way as he tried to train his bumbling apprentices in the skills of discipleship: "If any want to become my followers, let them deny themselves and take up their cross *daily* and follow me. For those who want to save their life will lose it, and those who lose their life for my sake will save it" (Luke 9:23-24).[2]

2. This essay by Chuck Campbell originally appeared in *Hospitality* 15 (October 1996): 4.

Dick Rustay and the Toilets[1]

DEUTERONOMY 5:12-15, EXODUS 20:8-11,
AND 1 CORINTHIANS 12:1-13

There's really only one place to begin this sermon — with Dick Rustay cleaning the toilets after the Butler Street Breakfast. Think about that image for a minute. Dick is a distinguished-looking gentleman, a partner here at the Open Door. He's a white man with a graduate-level education. He's an ordained pastor who has held numerous responsible positions. He could be working at a number of very respectable jobs. But each week when we go to the breakfast, Dick cleans the toilets. And I must confess, I have been impressed by Dick's willingness to grab the Ajax and the scrub brush and take on this task.

But a few weeks ago, Dick invited ME to clean the toilets with him. I was somewhat taken aback. I'm a seminary professor. And while I do clean the toilets at home, I've never cleaned toilets anywhere else. I certainly don't clean the toilets at the seminary. We hire other folks — poorer, less educated folks — to clean our toilets. I mean, what would it look like for a professor to be caught cleaning toilets at the seminary? And to clean up toilets after *homeless people* have used them. . . . Dick's invitation came as a bit of a shock to me.

But his invitation reminded me that an entire social system, in-

1. This sermon was preached by Chuck Campbell at the Open Door Community on September 14, 1997. The community requested a sermon dealing with a biblical understanding of work. Because Ed Loring was planning to preach the following week on keeping the Sabbath, I decided to look at the commandment from a different angle.

cluding an understanding of labor, is embodied in who cleans the toilets. Gandhi understood this. As one of his first acts of resistance to the social order in India, Gandhi began cleaning "toilets," a job that was rigidly reserved for people in the lowest caste. Simply by cleaning the "toilets" Gandhi began to turn the entire social order upside down. And he began to challenge the understanding of "work" inherent in that society.

That's why it's important for us to begin this evening with the image of Dick Rustay cleaning the toilets at Butler Street. That image gets us to a crucial aspect of a biblical view of work, which also offers a challenge to our social order and our understanding of labor.

The Bible doesn't really offer us a grand theory of work. It doesn't offer us a systematic theology of work or a detailed sociological analysis of labor. Rather, as we see in the Fourth Commandment, the Bible offers us a LOCATION — a place from which to view the matter. And that place is the location that Dick and others take when they clean the toilets at Butler Street. In Deuteronomy we are commanded, as a part of our Sabbath observance, to remember that "you were a slave in the land of Egypt." Observe the Sabbath week after week, the Fourth Commandment tells us, as a way of remembering your days in slavery. Do not consider the matter of work without remembering the time when you yourselves endured forced labor in Egypt. To look at work from that perspective will change your practices and transform your attitudes.

The Fourth Commandment reminds the people of Israel that the cries in Egypt were the cries of a people in forced labor. It reminds the people of Israel that the cries of slaves are at the heart of their story — and at the heart of our story. And these cries mingle today with other cries: the cries of poor people who clean toilets every night for minimum wage in our office buildings and hotels and sports arenas; the cries of men who suffer the inhumanity and injustice of the labor pools; the cry of the mill worker in a song by James Taylor. She sings:

> It's my life has been wasted, and I have been the fool
> To let this manufacturer use my body for a tool.
> I write home every evening staring at my hands,
> Swearing to my sorrow that a young girl ought to stand
>   a better chance.
> It's still me and my machine for the rest of the morning,

136

For the rest of the afternoon,
For the rest of my life.[2]

At the heart of our story as the people of God — at the heart of Sabbath observance — are these cries. The Fourth Commandment says, "Don't forget them. Stand *there* when you organize work."

For that is where God stands. The God of Israel, the God of Jesus, the God whose identity we know through the biblical story, stands with the workers, with those who endure forced labor, with those who clean the toilets. God doesn't recline up in heaven sipping wine and eating ambrosia. Rather, God hears the cries in Egypt, and God goes to work. God acts to liberate a huge pool of cheap, forced laborers from Egypt. God opens the doors of the labor pool office and says, "Let my people go!" And God's Word "happens"; the people are set free.

The Exodus is fundamentally about the liberation of people from dehumanizing work:

Work that offers no access to the means of production,
Work that provides no enjoyment of the fruits of our labors,
Work in which human labor becomes merely a cheap commodity
    to be used for the benefit of the wealthy and the powerful,
Work in which human beings become merely "manufacturers'
    tools."

God hears the cries of these laborers. And God brings them to a land of their own.

Where they can build their own houses and live in them,
Where they can plant their own gardens and enjoy the fruit of
    them,
Where human labor is not simply a cheap commodity, but a way
    of serving God, loving neighbor, and caring for creation.

So the Fourth Commandment states: whenever you worship, whenever you think about work, whenever you organize labor, re-

2. James Taylor, "Millworker," *James Taylor (Live)*, Columbia Records C2K 47056, 1993.

member all of this. Remember that you were slaves in Egypt. But remember also God's saving deeds. God liberates oppressed workers. God redeems human labor. God seeks meaningful, purposeful work for all people.

And remember, too, God's good creation, which is the focus of the Exodus version of the Fourth Commandment. God created work *good.* God created a world in which purposeful work is a vital part of life. At the time of creation, God placed human beings in the garden, not to sit around idle, but to tend the garden and keep it. Work is God's gracious gift to us. From the very beginning, we were created to work as a means of serving God and loving others and caring for creation.

One evening not long ago I was visiting with a man at the Central Presbyterian Church night shelter. I asked him what he had been doing during the day. "I did construction work through a labor pool," he told me. "What did they pay you?" I asked. "About twenty-five dollars," he replied. "I know I'm getting ripped off," he continued. "But I just can't sit around doing nothing all day. I *have* to work somewhere."

I learned what that man meant the first time I spent twenty-four hours on the street during Holy Week. I was expecting the experience to be dramatic and inspiring. I was looking forward to a new adventure at every turn. But instead, most of the time I was just bored. I had nothing to do. And finally, at one point, I broke the rules, got permission to leave the group, and spent a couple of hours doing volunteer work in the mail room at St. Luke's.[3] I even skipped lunch to get that "job." I'm not proud of what I did, but I learned a lot about the gift of work. And I began to understand why many of our friends on the streets choose to work, rather than eat.

The Fourth Commandment recognizes the human need for work. "Six days shall you labor," we read. But this command is not the same one we hear today from our legislators, who tell people on welfare, "Work — or else." "Work at these jobs that don't pay a living wage — or else." "Fill these positions that offer no health care benefits — or else." "Work at these jobs that we can't get anyone else to take — or

3. At the time this sermon was preached, St. Luke's Episcopal Church, in downtown Atlanta, offered numerous services to homeless people in the city, including a soup kitchen that served almost 500 people a day and a mail service that provided homeless people a place to pick up their mail. A friend of mine was the director of the mail room, and I asked him if I could help out during lunch.

else." Such threats are a distortion of the commandment, for God's commandments are not rigid rules to be imposed on people. Rather, they are statements about the crucial practices that are essential for a healthy community. And work, meaningful, living-wage work, is one of those practices. Any society with significant unemployment — or underemployment — is simply unacceptable to God.

Work is a gracious gift of God, created good and vital to human life in community. But the cries of slaves in Egypt and the cries of poor people today reveal the corruption of work by human sin. For all too many people work has become a way of slavery and death, rather than a means of life. And God simply cannot stand these corruptions. So God acts to bring slaves out of Egypt into a new community. And in his life, death, and resurrection, Jesus sets us free from the powers and systems that distort work and lead to oppression and death. And even now the Holy Spirit works for a new creation. The Spirit seeks to mold us into a new community that embodies an alternative to the ways of the world.

This is the kind of community that Paul holds before us in his letter to the Corinthians. Paul seeks to form a new community, which will embody a new organization of work.

> In this baptismal community social boundaries and hierarchies no longer function. Slave and free live together as equals, neither enjoying privileges denied to the other. So the cleaning of toilets can be shared, no longer a "menial chore" reserved for a class of "menial people."
>
> In this community everyone has distinctive, purposeful work that involves service to God, love of neighbor, and care of the creation.
>
> In this community everyone's work is valued and respected, because all work is a gift of the same Spirit.
>
> In this community work is done for the common good. For the Spirit is not one of competitive individualism, but a Spirit of cooperation and mutual love.
>
> And in this community, everyone shares in the fruits of labor.

At this table we embody and bear witness to this kind of community. For at this table the entire system of human labor is taken up into the way of Jesus and is judged and redeemed. Just think about it. At this table we find the agricultural industry that produced the grain and the grapes. We see the processing plants that transformed these raw products into bread and juice. Here, too, is the transportation system that brought the goods to the stores and the retail industry that marketed and sold the items to a customer. Here also are the manufacturing plants that made the trucks and trains, the construction industry that built the supermarkets, and the media that advertise the products. Here too are the government agencies that regulate and inspect all these industries. Here, in fact, is our entire economic system, political system, and legal system.[4]

Here at this table we find the entire social order and all who labor in it. And here at this table — miracle of miracles — all of this labor becomes a means to life, and everyone shares equally in the fruits!

There is no more subversive thing we can do than share this meal. For at this table we claim the entire social order, including the structure of labor, for the way of Jesus. And from this table — which was originally a Passover meal — Jesus sends us out to remember the cries of slaves in Egypt, to respond to the cries on the streets of Atlanta, and, of course, to clean the toilets at the Butler Street Breakfast.

4. This account of the Eucharist draws on Rafael Avila, *Worship and Politics*, trans. Alan Neely (Maryknoll, New York: Orbis Books, 1981), especially chapter 3. This sermon has also relied on M. Douglas Meeks's book, *God the Economist: The Doctrine of God and Political Economy* (Minneapolis: Fortress Press, 1989), especially chapter 6.

SPACE

So then you are no longer strangers and aliens, but you are citizens with the saints and also members of the household of God, built upon the foundation of the apostles and prophets, with Christ Jesus himself as the cornerstone. In him the whole structure is joined together and grows into a holy temple in the Lord; in whom you also are built together spiritually into a dwelling place for God.

EPHESIANS 2:19-22

A Dream about a Shelter

Etching with aquatint; 24" × 18"; © 1999 Christina Bray

On Tall Buildings and Forgetting God[1]

Each year during the annual celebration of the Festival of Shelters, the Open Door Community and its friends worship together in Woodruff Park in downtown Atlanta. When we stand here in the park and take in the scenery around us, we see, as in any modern American city, the tall buildings all around us, the steel, glass, and concrete that make this city a city. If we look more closely amidst all those hard edges, we are likely to begin seeing the symbols of human hope and despair.

In human mythologies, tall buildings are one of the nearly universal symbols of human pride and achievement. They represent not only the technological ability to pack a lot of people and things into an area with a relatively small footprint, but also the pinnacle of human aspiration and accomplishment. This is especially true in modern American culture, where bigness is one of our idols.

Our city buildings are also mechanisms of social control. Construction of one of these behemoths nearly always requires displacing some people from their homes. We also employ, often at slave wages, the least ones of our society to clear the space and construct the buildings. But once construction is finished, the builders often find that they are excluded from using what they have crafted. And if you manage to get past the security guards in one of the towers and make it onto an

---

1. This meditation was given by Stan Saunders in Woodruff Park at a worship gathering during the Festival of Shelters, September 1996. It later appeared in *Hospitality* 16 (September 1997): 1-2.

elevator, you are likely to find that access to this or that floor is denied. You see, each of the buildings tells a story of who is in and who is out, who has power and who does not, who is welcome and who is not.

The tall buildings we see all around us are also symbols of the modern spiritual quest. Why do humans build spaces like skyscrapers, after all? For one thing, they give us a sense of permanence and control over our environment; they suggest to us that, within their walls and looking down from their heights, the world is not such a threatening place. They suggest to us that we have the means to shape a world that we can control and manipulate. And isn't this idea — that we have the right and the ability to shape and control our world — at the heart of human spiritualities, especially in their modern American expressions?

This is not really a new insight, however. Remember that one of the first human responses to the fall in Genesis was to start building cities, a burst of human creativity that culminated in the Tower of Babel, the ultimate symbol of human pride. What the Genesis story tells us, in other words, is that cities are human attempts to respond to the consequences of the fall; they are shrines to the powers of this world. We build cities and tall buildings because we are no longer in fellowship with God. One might even argue that, as a principle, the greater the buildings we see around us, the deeper the sense of underlying despair, fear, and alienation. From a biblical standpoint we can put the issue this way: cities are danger zones for human beings, because they tempt us to celebrate our own accomplishment, to construct our own realities, and to forget who God is and what God wants to do for us.

Forgetfulness is the name of the game in urban politics in Atlanta these days. When the city leaders and local press wage war against the poor and the homeless, they are pressing battle to make us forget that all we have comes from God. They are seeking to make the picture of downtown more comfortable and attractive for the "right kinds of folks." Polishing the idols, as it were. The risk in all this is that, when we have sufficiently sanitized the city of unsavory citizens, we will forget the pain and suffering of those we have put away. We will put up bigger walls, install better security systems, and celebrate our ingenuity. We may even be tempted to give thanks to God for not making us like those people on the outside. We may think that our world of idols is the way God meant it to be. But the only way we could think all these things is if we have forgotten who our God is. To embrace the city our leaders have in mind is to forget that life is lived most faithfully in trusting relationship with a merciful and loving God, a God who has promised to give us what we need to live today.

The consequences of such forgetfulness should be well known to those who read the Bible. Deuteronomy 8, among many other texts, spells this out with great clarity:

> Take care that you do not forget the LORD your God, by failing to keep his commandments, his ordinances, and his statutes, which I am commanding you today. When you have eaten your fill and have built fine houses and live in them, and when your herds and flocks have multiplied, and your silver and gold is multiplied, and all that you have is multiplied, then do not exalt yourself, forgetting the LORD your God, who brought you out of the land of Egypt, out of the house of slavery, who led you through the great and terrible wilderness, an arid wasteland with poisonous snakes and scorpions. He made water flow for you from flint rock, and fed you in the wilderness with manna that your ancestors did not know, to humble you and to test you, and in the end to do you good. Do not say to yourself, "My power and the might of my own hand have gotten me this wealth." But remember the LORD your God, for it is he who gives you power to get wealth, so that he may confirm his covenant that he swore to your ancestors, as he is doing today. If you do forget the LORD your God and follow other gods to serve and worship them, I solemnly warn you today that you shall surely perish. Like the nations that the LORD is destroying before you, so shall you perish, because you would not obey the voice of the LORD your God. (8:11-20)

It was in order to avoid such forgetfulness that the Festival of Shelters was first introduced to the people of Israel so long ago. During the festival, the people were not to live in their houses, but in the little huts and tents that were a reminder to them of their origins as a wandering, wilderness people, a people who lived in the promises of God rather than in a land of their own devising. The prophet Zechariah closes his visions of judgment against the nations with a warning that they, too, are to attend to the Festival of Shelters. Year after year the nations are to go up to Jerusalem to worship God and to join the Festival of Booths (or Shelters). If they do not, Zechariah promises that they will have no rain. If Egypt does not go up to join the festival, they will be visited with the plagues God has reserved for the nations (Zechariah 14:16-19).

That is why we, a tiny rag-tag community, gather each year in the heart of Atlanta's tall buildings. Our calling as Christians is to remember who God is, what God has done for us, and what God wants to do for us. We have to gather in the middle of the city because, in the midst of all the shrines of human accomplishment and forgetfulness, someone needs to make sure there will be rain. So, we come here amidst all the marvelous buildings because we remember that God is the one who brought us out of the wilderness, who preserves our life, and who gives us what we need today. We gather in Woodruff Park to remember God and in this way to gain discernment and vision for our ongoing journey towards God's redemption of the world.

While we're on the streets of the city during the Festival of Shelters, we also listen to the stories of our brothers and sisters who have been cast aside and crushed under the machinery of the city builders. In doing so we continue not only the tradition of remembering what is embodied in the Festival of Shelters, but also the foundational Christian tradition of hospitality and solidarity with the poor, the homeless — the resident aliens (1 Peter 2:11) and exiles of this world. The streets are where the gospel story can most clearly and powerfully be heard, and where God can most clearly be seen. In our comfortable homes and our towering offices, the gospel may not make much sense, if we can hear it at all. In the middle of the city there is both danger and opportunity. We must be wary lest the grandeur of human accomplishment, the monuments of pride, blur our vision and cloud our memory. In the city we may be greatly tempted to forget God. But amidst all these symbols of human hope and despair, we have the possibility of witnessing God at work, knitting together a fresh creation. God grant us eyes to see and ears to hear.

Sweet Security

The security business must be booming. Everywhere I go, it seems, uniformed — and often armed — security guards are there. When I go to the bank, I enter past a security guard. In the shopping malls and grocery stores security guards abound. Businesses, restaurants, and hotels employ them. Woodruff Park is swarming with them. At the seminary where I teach, a security guard occasionally pokes his head into my office to make sure everything's okay. And security guards are not just limited to these places where we might expect them. I recently attended a youth soccer tournament, and there, at the entrance to the parking lot, was an armed security guard. And when I go to worship on Sunday I am often greeted by a uniformed guard. Ironically, as our prisons grow more and more crowded, many of us feel less and less secure on the streets, in the stores, even at church. Security guards are becoming an accepted part of life.

As a privileged white male, I experience very little threat from these security personnel. They don't look suspiciously at me or give me any hassle. In fact, they are usually cordial, pleasant people. I simply don't fall into the category of persons they have been told to watch for and guard against. Indeed, I am one of those persons the guards seek to make feel safe and secure. The security guards present no real problem for me personally. Maybe that's why they are so easily becoming an accepted part of life; they pose no threat to people in power.

I often wonder, however, what these guards look like from the perspective of a black man in our society. I wonder how the guards appear to poor people — black or white or Hispanic or Asian — who may not be dressed very well or smell very good. What is it like to be looked at suspiciously by a guard every time you turn around? What is it like to feel uncomfortable or threatened when you walk into a store or hang out at a park or enter a church? What is it like to live in a world of security guards when you are the one being "watched," when you are the "suspect," simply because of the color of your skin or the clothes you wear? It's hard for me to imagine security guards as the "enemy" — just as it was hard for me to imagine the police as the "enemy" until I was placed under arrest one night in Woodruff Park. However, such is the reality for many homeless people I have talked to. And from this perspective, security guards are disturbing symbols of the racism and classism that pervades our society.

Which makes what is happening at the Sweet Auburn Curb Market even more remarkable.[1] Every night the management of the market allows — indeed welcomes — about twenty-five homeless men and women to sleep against the west wall of the building under a protective awning. The police have been notified and do not hassle the homeless folks who gather there. Indeed, the market even provides a place for the men and women to store their belongings during the day. On some evenings, church groups bring food for the small homeless community. And one evening each week, people come to lead worship at the market. For their part, the homeless people agree to keep the area clean and to urinate in designated places.

I learned about this odd arrangement during Holy Week, when I slept at the market during one of the Open Door's twenty-four-hour vigils. As I discovered the details of the arrangement, I became curious. Why does the market welcome homeless men and women at the very time when most of downtown seems to be trying to secure itself against them? Why does the market view these people not as threats, but as friends? The answer came as a complete surprise: SECURITY! The market, I discovered, had been having break-ins on the west side of the building. So the management invited the homeless men and

---

1. The Sweet Auburn Curb Market is located down the block from Grady Hospital and across the street from the Butler Street C.M.E. Church, where the Open Door Community used to serve the Butler Street Breakfast. It is, in short, part of the "contested space" in the Grady Hospital area.

women to make that space their home. And because of the presence of the homeless community, the break-ins have stopped.

Like Jesus, the Sweet Auburn Market has turned the world on its head. While most of downtown lives in fear of homeless people and guards itself against them, the market has sought security not *against* homeless people, but *alongside* them. Whenever I pass a security guard now, I remember the Sweet Auburn Market. Maybe real security lies not in uniformed guards, but in hospitality, relationships, jobs, and homes.[2]

2. This essay by Chuck Campbell originally appeared in *Hospitality* 16 (July 1997): 3. Unfortunately, a week after it was written, the managers of the Sweet Auburn Curb Market stopped allowing homeless people to sleep against the wall of their building.

It's a Zoo Out There?

Last year during Holy Week I had the unusual opportunity to spend twenty-four hours on the streets with the Open Door Community *and* a night at the Atlanta Zoo with my son's fourth-grade class. I learned a lot about Atlanta and our society through these two experiences.

The twenty-four-hour street experience began on Sunday evening, March 31, as our group left 910 around 7:30 and walked downtown in a chilly drizzle. By the time we had gotten to Butler Street, the drizzle had changed into a light rain, so we stopped for a while on a covered sidewalk outside Grady Memorial Hospital. Knowing that we would not be allowed to remain there for the night, we soon left and went up to the Capitol area to look for a dry place to sleep. The only shelter we could find was a concrete vault housing a dumpster behind Central Presbyterian Church. But that place was taken. In the shadows of the vault, amidst the stench of the dumpster, we noticed a homeless man sleeping on the lone "bed" — a concrete ledge on the side of the vault. It was the only dry space available.

Finally, we came to rest back on Butler Street at the covered entrance to the Fulton County Health Department. We squeezed in alongside other "urban campers," packed like sardines in that small space. Although the rain soon stopped, many other homeless people came by the building that night seeking a dry place to sleep. They had to keep moving, however. There was no room at this "inn."

After a restless night, I woke up shivering and needing to pee around 4:00 A.M. Because there were no toilet facilities available, I

150

broke the law and urinated on a grassy area behind the health department building. Then I quickly paced back and forth in front of the building trying to get warm. Around 5:00 the rest of our group arose, and we began a long day. We visited a labor pool, where exhausted men sold their last ounces of energy to work for sub-living wages. We stood in lines for hours waiting for meals — only one of which (the Butler Street Breakfast) was balanced and nutritious. We also visited the Municipal Court, where homeless people are daily charged with various violations, many, such as public urination, related to the necessities of homelessness. As a cold front moved in and the weather turned frigid, I asked several men, "Where will you sleep tonight?" "I don't know" was the answer I received most often. "The winter shelters closed last night." One man, still wearing his wristband from Grady Hospital, moved very slowly, wondering where he could get the rest he needed to continue his recovery. At the end of the day I returned home physically and emotionally exhausted, my eyes once again opened to the realities of homelessness in Atlanta.

Three days later I loaded up my van with fourth graders for an overnight trip to the Atlanta Zoo. After arriving at the zoo, we gathered in an educational building to see and touch a variety of small animals. Gently removing the animals from various containers, the trainers brought them to us one by one. "Please treat the animals with care," we were told. "Don't make any sudden movements. You might scare the hedgehog." "Don't press too hard on the hissing beetle. You might injure it."

After this engaging educational period, we toured the zoo itself, a truly magical place after dark, with peacocks resting in the trees, their loud screeches piercing the air. We were shown the impressive facilities where the animals are housed, including the provisions available for cold weather. We saw the nursery where newborns are cared for, and the infirmary where sick animals are nursed back to health. The next day, we discovered, there would be no outside elephant show because the elephants would be receiving their indoor baths.

Most impressive, however, was the food building, an enormous structure devoted to storing and preparing the animals' meals. There seemed to be every kind of food imaginable: frozen chicks and rats for the small carnivores, red steaks for the lions and tigers, raw vegetables for the "vegetarians," grains of every kind imaginable, and even vitamins to insure proper nutrition. On spotless stainless-steel tables lay thick notebooks detailing every dietary requirement for each animal in the zoo. I had never realized the enormous resources, expertise, and love required to operate a zoo and care for the animals. I went home the next day impressed by the knowledge and commitment of the zoo staff.

At times I have heard people say of downtown Atlanta, "It's a real zoo out there." After Holy Week last year, I can only reply, "I wish!"[1]

1. This essay by Chuck Campbell originally appeared in *Hospitality* 16 (April 1997): 9.

Discipleship of the Body

In his book, *The Identity of Jesus Christ*, the theologian Hans Frei wrote the following: ". . . the embodiment of the Easter story's pattern in our lives means . . . a new way of governing our *bodies*. That is how we are in touch with the story."[1] I have cited Frei's words many times. Only recently, however, have I begun to grasp their importance. While working as an apprentice with the folks at Urban Training Organization and the Open Door Community, I have come to realize that my teachers repeatedly direct me simply to place my *body* in new and different spaces.

"Take your body out of the air-conditioned calm and comfort of Columbia Seminary," the people at Urban Training told me. "Put your body instead in a couple of Atlanta's public housing projects. Go and sweat in the stifling heat of the Herndon Homes Community Center and become dizzy amidst the chaotic lives of the young men who meet there. Go sit in the apartment of a teenage mother at Perry Homes [where an infant recently choked to death on a cockroach]. Place your body in these locations, and learn there about the privilege of your 'white' flesh."

"Move your body out of your large home and your warm bed," folks at the Open Door told me, "and place it on the streets of Atlanta for twenty-four hours. Sleep (or try to) on the cold concrete and wake

---

1. Hans W. Frei, *The Identity of Jesus Christ: The Hermeneutical Bases of Dogmatic Theology* (Philadelphia: Fortress Press, 1975), p. 171.

up shivering. Look unsuccessfully for a toilet to use — and don't forget you can be arrested for relieving yourself elsewhere. Stand in line for hours for your meals, stomach growling. Walk the streets all day. Experience, in a small way, the urgency and exhaustion of homeless people — in your body."

And there was more. "Put your body in the waiting room at the Grady Infectious Disease Clinic. Sit with people who have AIDS as they wait to have their bodies pricked and poked and prodded. And don't miss, sitting next to you, the sick prisoner, his body clothed in an orange jumpsuit, his ankles in shackles, his wrists in handcuffs. Then go down to the pharmacy and wait for medicine — over an hour for a bottle of aspirin. In your tense muscles, feel how poor people pay with their time if not their money.

"Take your body into the Fulton County Jail. Visit with inmates through a pane of glass, unable even to shake hands. Notice the lipstick marks on the glass, the residue of kisses which fell short of human lips — each one a cry for physical contact with a husband or lover. And take your body to death row in Jackson. Pass through a barred, electronic gate, a metal detector, another set of bars, and another, and another. Then, finally inside, hug death row inmates — and receive their hugs. Experience in your body the isolation and humanity of people scheduled for electrocution.

"Walk your body into a labor pool, under the suspicious gaze of the 'foreman' because you're too white and too clean and too rested. Sit on the hard, wooden benches and feel your back begin to ache. Breathe the smoke-filled air, and smell the hardworking men who have no place to shower. Wonder what it's like to be treated as little more than a body — as a mere physical, human tool in the service of Atlanta's corporate greed."

At a time when the church seems obsessed with "spirituality" and seminaries offer degrees in "spiritual formation," my mentors at Urban Training and the Open Door have taught me the deep truth of Hans Frei's words: ". . . the embodiment of the Easter story's pattern in our lives means . . . a new way of governing our *bodies*. That is how we are in touch with the story." When someone recently asked me to share some ways I nurture my spiritual life, my immediate response surprised me: "Over the past year," I replied, "my spiritual life has been shaped most by what I've been doing with my *body*." At first, that reply seemed like a paradox: spiritual formation is directly related to the discipleship of the body. But then I remembered Paul's words: ". . . present your bodies as a living sacrifice, holy and acceptable to God, which is your spiritual worship" (Romans 12:1). And I remembered that the story of Jesus begins with the incarnation and moves toward the resurrection of the *body*. The surprise and paradox disappeared. As Hans Frei and Urban Training and the Open Door have taught me, we get in touch with *this* story through our bodies.[2]

2. This essay by Chuck Campbell originally appeared in *Hospitality* 15 (August 1996): 5.

"Justice Is Important, but Supper Is Essential": Solidarity, Hospitality, and Urban Spirituality

The will to give ourselves to others and "welcome" them, to re-adjust our identities to make space for them, is prior to any judgment about others, except that of identifying them in their humanity. The will to embrace precedes any "truth" about others and any construction of their "justice." This will is absolutely indiscriminate and strictly immutable; it transcends the moral mapping of the social world into "good" and "evil."[1]

What should be the church's response to the poor and oppressed? . . . [The question itself reveals] a belief that "the church" is something quite separate from the "poor and oppressed"; they are two different things responding to each other, rather than one and the same thing. When the church is not seen as rooted in and identified with the broken ones, then the poor and oppressed are clearly outsiders, and the only response . . . will of course be condescending, paternalistic charity.[2]

1. Miroslav Volf, *Exclusion and Embrace: A Theological Exploration of Identity, Otherness, and Reconciliation* (Nashville: Abingdon Press, 1996), p. 29.
2. Louis Smith and Joseph Barndt, *Beyond Brokenness* (New York: Friendship Press, 1980), p. 108, cited in Michael Elliott, *Why the Homeless Don't Have Homes and What to Do About It* (Cleveland: Pilgrim Press, 1993), p. 66.

Poor People, Moral Maps, and Space

"The problem is space." So says our friend Ed Loring of the Open Door Community. "Poor people are having space taken away from them." Urban camping ordinances, the absence of public toilets, the police sweeps before large public events, the new gates and fences all over town (even around churches), the security guards at the door (even church doors), and the constant pressure on the homeless just to move on — all of these provide cold, hard evidence that he is right. These realities, along with welfare reform, the loss of affordable housing, and the lack of affordable health care, comprise the arsenal for Atlanta's (and America's) undeclared war on the poor.

Even more than removing poor people from the public dole, the goal of this war seems primarily to remove poor and homeless people from sight. One of the quickest means to this end is simply to devise new grounds for arresting and imprisoning the poorest of the poor. The federal government, states, and many large cities in the United States are putting a lot of energy, creativity, and, ironically, no little expense into this effort. At a time when we are seeking to reduce our spending on poverty programs and "end welfare as we know it," and at a time when the number of affordable housing units in our cities is decreasing, we are spending more than ever to build prisons and jails. Immediately preceding the 1996 Olympic Games, three new jails were built in Atlanta by Dekalb County, Fulton County, and the City of Atlanta. The construction workers hired through the labor pools to help build these facilities made wry jokes, as we have noted before, that they were building the "hotels" where they would be staying during the games. As a nation, we now have 1.8 million people behind bars, more than any other country in the world, except perhaps Russia. Even communist China, whose population is nearly five times greater than our own, has probably half a million fewer people in prison than do we.[3] In short, we are indeed creating space for the poor — out of sight in our prisons.[4]

3. Eric Schlosser, "The Prison-Industrial Complex," *The Atlantic Monthly* 282, no. 6 (December 1998): 53. See also Joe Davidson, "Caged Cargo," *Emerge* (October 1997): 36-46; and Harmon Wray, "Dungeons for Dollars? The Trend Toward Prisons for Profit," *Hospitality* 18, no. 1 (January 1999): 1-2.

4. We now spend approximately $35 billion annually on the "corrections" element of the criminal-justice budget. Since 1991 the rate of violent crime has fallen

The problem is not really that there isn't enough space for everyone, but that so many of us are either unwilling or don't know how to share space fully and freely with those around us. Perhaps this is so because those who embody our economic and social nightmares threaten us. Media images and stereotypes of poor and homeless people also play a role in the creation of our attitudes by objectifying and vilifying a wide range of people who are more often victims than victimizers.[5]

The resistance North Americans have to sharing space with poor people — and the difficulties poor people have in claiming space to share — also have roots in our cultural assumptions about personhood, private property, and privilege. In this culture, ownership of land, houses, cars, and other possessions is a primary means for the expression of identity. With property comes power; ownership makes one a person to be reckoned with. When we lose the resources to purchase property, we also lose voice, political presence, and the capacity to construct "personal space" and define our own identity. Those who have power express it not only in the private realm, however, but pub-

---

by 20 percent, while the number of people in prison and jail has risen by 50 percent. See Schlosser, "The Prison-Industrial Complex," p. 54. Schlosser's statistics on the demographics of the prison population are also revealing: "The raw material of the prison-industrial complex is its inmates: the poor, the homeless, and the mentally ill; drug dealers, drug addicts, alcoholics, and a wide assortment of violent sociopaths. About 70 percent of the prison inmates in the United States are illiterate. Perhaps 200,000 of the country's inmates (over 10 percent) suffer from a serious mental illness. A generation ago such people were handled primarily by the mental-health, not the criminal-justice, system. . . . Although the prevalence of illegal drug use among white men is approximately the same as that among black men, black men are five times as likely to be arrested for a drug offense. As a result, about half the inmates in the United States are African-American. One out of every fourteen black men is now in prison or jail. One out of every four black men is likely to be imprisoned at some point during his lifetime. The number of women sentenced to a year or more of prison has grown twelve-fold since 1970. Of the 80,000 women now imprisoned, about 70 percent are nonviolent offenders. About 75 percent have children."

5. For a discussion of the ways language and media images have shaped our perceptions of poor people, and thus also public policy, see Herbert J. Gans, *The War Against the Poor: The Underclass and Antipoverty Policy* (New York: Basic Books, 1995). The racial aspects of American poverty policy are analyzed by Martin Gilens, *Why Americans Hate Welfare* (Chicago: University of Chicago Press, 1999).

licly. This helps explain why struggles over space so often come to expression around attempts to define and control the use of public space, as illustrated by the disputes in Atlanta over the use of Woodruff Park, to cite but one example. The outcomes of these disputes almost without exception serve the interests of the business community and the better-off members of the society, who perceive in the presence of homeless people a misuse of public space and a threat to their own safety, freedom, and privacy.

If poor people cannot afford to purchase space of their own, and if they are also denied the use of public space, where can they turn to find space to live? Putting the matter in these terms may help us see that issues concerning the use of public spaces by poor and homeless people are not merely about public safety or economic development — the terms in which they are usually presented — but foundational *moral* issues. Questions of how human beings will share space have to do not only with the most basic aspects of our polity, but with the very character of our life together as God's children. Our construction of physical and social space reflects and subsequently shapes the construction of our corporate — and individual — soul. The physical spaces and social arrangements we construct around us, in other words, have to do with the space in our hearts — space for both the stranger and for God.[6] What, then, are we to do with the "stranger" at our door?

Closing the Door

On the one hand, we can simply close the door, as we do when we send so many poor people to jail, essentially because they are homeless. The racial and socio-economic segregation that characterizes Atlanta's urban and suburban arrangements is yet another expression of closing the door, and a fairly typical response to the threat the "stranger" poses for members of mainstream North American society.

6. Miroslav Volf's book, *Exclusion and Embrace,* cited above, offers a rich analysis of the ways we are taught to shape identity exclusively, as well as a solid theological foundation for turning from exclusion to embrace. See also Judith M. Gundry-Volf and Miroslav Volf, *A Spacious Heart: Essays on Identity and Belonging* (Harrisburg, Pennsylvania: Trinity Press International, 1997).

Closing the door offers the immediate advantage of removing the perceived problem from sight and mind.

But what if the stranger keeps on knocking? And what are we to do when we need to leave the security of our space behind the closed door? Having closed the door physically, we are likely to seek to keep it closed psychically. Thus, even as the economy has "boomed" in places like Atlanta, we have grown less tolerant of the visible human wreckage, perhaps for its potential to disturb our carefully nurtured sense of security and success.[7] So, we continue to build segregated, gated developments and install security systems in our homes, we build more prisons and jails, and, increasingly, we carry deadly weapons for our own "protection."

If any of these measures actually worked, Americans should be feeling better. Yet, as our isolation increases, so too does our anxiety, along with our willingness to resort to ever more extreme measures to preserve a sense of security. All of these expressions of closing the door and keeping it closed — the "solutions" our society continues to pursue to address the threats of poverty and violence — in fact offer no real solution at all. Closing the door simply perpetuates the attitudes and actions that have generated the problem in the first place.

Our willingness to keep the door closed and our growing capacity to look the other way when confronted by poverty in the public sphere lead us to accept not only the segregation of our neighborhoods and public places, but also the segregation of our consciousness and being. When we close the door or turn away from the stranger, a door closes within us, as well. Whether by crossing the street to avoid a bag lady or a homeless person, or by voting to reduce the capital gains tax while also eliminating social programs for poor people, or by locking our car doors as we drive through certain parts of town, we endow the fragmentation and corrosion of our own spirit and being. Ultimately, continuing to close the door to the stranger rends the fabric of our own soul, as well as the society in which we seek to live.

7. Gans, *The War Against the Poor*, pp. 58-102, provides an insightful analysis of the ways our economic arrangements, social institutions, and even language legitimate the interests and self-understanding of the privileged at the expense of the "undeserving poor."

The Church and Closing Doors

Despite genuine concern among Christians for poor and homeless people, and despite countless sermons calling us to advocacy on behalf of the poor, we cannot but confess that the church's engagement with poor people is at best spotty. About a third of the congregations in Atlanta report some level of involvement in providing housing or shelter for the homeless.[8] If pressed to choose, many congregations prefer to send money to support mission and benevolence in other parts of the world, rather than address the needs of homeless people living nearby. Why? American Christians tend to share with their non-Christian counterparts a culturally based moral disdain for poor people.[9] The individualism that is so prevalent in American culture leads us to believe that each member of the society is responsible for his or her financial welfare, rather than part of a complex web of economic relationships and forces that few of us can control. We also tend to believe that the "business of the church" is religion, not economics. In any case, those who seek to elicit greater compassion and involvement among Christians on behalf of poor people must fight against powerful cultural stereotypes and biases, sometimes even against religiously motivated bias.

Even if more Christians shared a clear understanding of the nature of poverty in the United States and were more willing to put convictions into action, it is not clear how much congregations would or could do. The social construction of congregations in North American culture clearly leans toward socially homogenous enclaves, distinguished by racial and socio-economic aspects as well as by denominational affiliation. Most congregations exist as self-standing institutions, with their own self-enclosed meeting spaces, thereby possessing the qualities of a "private association." In keeping with these social and spatial arrangements, most congregations direct their expressions of solidarity or hospitality primarily at their own membership, or at potential members (usually "people like us"). Engagement with poor

---

8. Elliott, *Why the Homeless Don't Have Homes*, p. 64, citing an article in the *Atlanta Journal-Constitution*, April 19, 1992.

9. See Robert Wuthnow, "What Religious People Think About the Poor," *The Christian Century* (September 7-14, 1994): 812-16.

or homeless people is usually understood as a form of benevolence, that is, as an act of charity rather than an opportunity to build a relationship. Thus, even congregations that provide services and financial support for poor and homeless people tend to resist actually including such persons in their fellowship.

The physical location of congregations makes some difference in their responses to poor and homeless people, but both suburban and inner-city congregations resist moving beyond charity to fellowship and solidarity, albeit for different reasons. Many predominantly white, "mainstream" denominational congregations in the suburbs of Atlanta are made up of people who fled downtown areas as they felt the encroachment of "urban blight." Because of their physical location, as well as their socio-economic inclinations, these congregations are less likely to encounter large numbers of homeless people on their doorsteps, and thus would have to go out of their way to nurture genuine practices of hospitality and solidarity with poor people even if they were so inclined.

On the other hand, the predominantly white congregations in central Atlanta that have survived and flourished typically take the form of commuter congregations; they are located in the city, but draw their membership from the suburbs. They are, then, sociocultural and economic islands in an environment that often seems threatening and hostile. While such congregations are more likely to establish support programs for the poor and homeless around them, those who are served rarely join the congregation that gathers on Sunday.[10] Although the physical distance between the congregants and the poor is reduced in some instances, the social barriers usually remain in place.

In both suburban and inner-city congregations, then, segregation along racial, economic, and class lines is the prevailing norm. In this way the church replicates the patterns of segregation that are typical of the larger society. Even when the doors are opened for the poor, the terms of engagement are nonetheless usually dictated by the interests of the insiders. Because of this, the ways to solidarity remain blocked. As Michael Elliott puts it, "The single greatest sign most congregations give to the homeless is locked doors. For the homeless, these buildings

---

10. See the description of the typical "old first" church in Elliott, *Why the Homeless Don't Have Homes*, pp. 62ff.

are often painful reminders they are not wanted, even by those who claim to care for them."[11]

If the physical and social construction of space among Christian congregations is an impediment to establishing bonds of friendship and solidarity with poor people, so, too, the "social construction" of our worship services plays a key role. While we talk a lot about and pray for justice, peace, reconciliation, forgiveness of debts, and even hospitality, the design of our worship gatherings is not particularly well suited to the actual practice of any of these disciplines of the Spirit. Many of our patterns of worship are legacies of "Christendom," when Christianity was the rule of the land and good citizenship (i.e., social conformity) served as the functional definition of discipleship. Much of our worship, thus, consists of carefully choreographed, uniform behavior — standing up together, sitting down together, singing and speaking in unison — all driven by custom and directed by authority figures. Where in this worship paradigm is there real opportunity to practice forgiving and being forgiven our debts, or for forging reconciled relationships with strangers? For the most part, apparently, the actual practice of these disciplines must happen in some other social space and at some other time.

In short, the "social construction" of many North American congregations is not conducive, and often resistant, to the spiritual and missionary disciplines that could facilitate making and maintaining a different kind of social space for the poor and homeless people among us. Given our cultural affinity for the use of doors as barriers, what would be required of us were we to choose, on the other hand, to open the door and join our lives with the poorest of the poor?

As we have walked the streets, listened to Scripture, and looked for signs of God's presence on the streets of Atlanta during the last few years, we have only just begun to learn what it means to think and act outside the constructs supplied by the powers that be in cities like Atlanta. Resisting the powers is not easy. But we are convinced that the way things are is not the way things have to be. We assert this, first, because we believe God's presence in the world is always transformative, shattering the conventional wisdom of the world and subjecting the powers of this world to God's loving will. Second, the arrange-

11. Elliott, *Why the Homeless Don't Have Homes*, p. 61.

ment of social space is always a "human construct," that is, something humans invent (or, more often, to which they give tacit consent). And if our current arrangements are social constructions, they can be torn down and rebuilt. The way things are is not the way things have to be.

As Christians, we believe that real transformation only happens when God acts and when, as a consequence, God's people begin to discern reality and shape their practices outside the paradigms supplied by our society. God has entered the world in Jesus Christ, we confess, and because of this, all of reality is being transformed — "If anyone is in Christ, there is a new creation" (2 Corinthians 5:17). As they heard and responded to the good news of Jesus Christ, the early Christians found themselves drawn together in communities that were focused on and enlivened by the reconciling Spirit of God. People who would never sit together as equals in the society around them now sat together at one table as sisters and brothers. By performing the gospel story at table and within households, that is, within the social structures and spaces mediated to them by their culture, they worked toward the transformation of those structures, focusing particularly on practices of solidarity and hospitality, welcoming strangers and enemies into their midst.

What then would be required of Christians and of the churches in order to begin to transform the spaces in which we live and work in cities like Atlanta? What could we do to "contest the spaces" where segregation, alienation, and violence are the norm, and where our construction of social and physical space deprives poor people of life and dignity? How would we need to refocus our spiritual and missional practices in order to realize the peace of Jesus Christ among the poor in a city like Atlanta?

Solidarity, Hospitality, and the Reconstruction of Social Space

Our experiences on the streets in Atlanta have taught us again and again that the answers to these questions begin and end in the disciplines of hospitality and solidarity. If you were to ask most Christians in North America today to name the most important spiritual disciplines, hospitality and solidarity are likely to occur far down the list, if they are named at all. Nor are these terms prominent in the lexicon of missionary priorities in most congregations. But the practices these terms designate are very prominent in the pages of the New Testament. Why the discrepancy? Why are these terms so infrequently a part of the vocabulary of North American Christians?

Part of the answer may lie in the countless shifts that have taken place across the history of the church, particular those having to do with the movement of the Christian faith into modern Western culture. Because we have learned to shape identity in individual terms, we have also come to think of the Christian faith as a religion having to do primarily with the relationship between God and the individual soul. In this framework, spiritual disciplines have taken on a distinctly personal and individual flavor; spirituality is for us the most personal aspect of our already individualistic approach to religion. Thus, more communally oriented concepts and practices, such as solidarity and hospitality, can seem like curiosities, at best. In the world of the New Testament, however, individually oriented approaches to identity would have been considered anomalous, while group-oriented understandings of identity, salvation, and even ethics were the norm.[12]

Given the orientation toward group-oriented identity in Mediterranean culture, it is not surprising that hospitality was a highly regarded social convention in the world of the New Testament, as it still is in many parts of the world today. The Greek word we translate as "hospitality" literally means "love for the stranger," designating those practices that draw the stranger into my group or family. As John Koenig puts it, among ancient Greek and near-Eastern peoples, hospitality was concerned with a "sacred bond between guests and hosts"; it was "one of the pillars of morality upon which the universe stands." He goes on to note that the New Testament witnesses developed this tradition by emphasizing "the presence of God or Christ in ordinary

12. On the group orientation of the New Testament world, see especially Bruce J. Malina, *The New Testament World: Insights from Cultural Anthropology,* rev. ed. (Louisville: Westminster/John Knox Press, 1993), pp. 63-89; Bruce J. Malina and Jerome H. Neyrey, *Portraits of Paul: An Archaeology of Ancient Personality* (Louisville: Westminster/John Knox Press, 1996), pp. 10-18, 154-76; Gerhard Lohfink, *Jesus and Community: The Social Dimension of Christian Faith* (Philadelphia: Fortress Press, 1984); and Carolyn Osiek and David Balch, *Families in the New Testament World: Households and House Churches* (Louisville: Westminster/John Knox Press, 1997).

exchanges between human guests and hosts."[13] We see the New Testament emphasis on hospitality with particular clarity in the countless discussions of and stories about table fellowship, both in the Gospels and Acts and in Paul's letters, to which we will return below.

If we understand "sacramental space" as those places and events where divine and human activity coincide,[14] then the move to understanding hospitality both as a foundational spiritual discipline and as a tool for the reconstitution of human space becomes obvious. In hospitality we are brought close both to the stranger and to God. In hospitality the dividing walls of hostility fall down (cf. Ephesians 2:14-16; Romans 15:7ff.) and a new creation comes into being. In hospitality we open the door and invite the stranger in, the lines between guest and host blur (cf. Luke 24:13-34), and we discern and celebrate God's reconciling presence. Koenig argues that in the New Testament, the word for hospitality denotes not just a love of strangers, but "a delight in the whole guest-host relationship."[15] This relationship is powerfully transforming. Though always threatening and disorienting, the practice and celebration of hospitality generates new ways of perceiving the world and new social configurations, as well as new awareness of the dimensions of God's presence. The practices of hospitality, thus, also blur the boundaries between two disciplines we usually separate, spirituality and mission, both of which are concerned ultimately with the discovery of God's transforming presence in the world.

The same can also be said with regard to "solidarity,"[16] for hospi-

---

13. John Koenig, *New Testament Hospitality: Partnership with Strangers as Promise and Mission* (Philadelphia: Fortress Press, 1985), p. 2. Other important studies of hospitality include Thomas Olgetree, *Hospitality to the Stranger: Dimensions of Moral Understanding* (Philadelphia: Fortress Press, 1985); Parker Palmer, *The Company of Strangers: Christians and the Renewal of America's Public Life* (New York: Crossroad, 1981).

14. Following John Howard Yoder, *Body Politics: Five Practices of the Christian Community Before the Watching World* (Nashville: Discipleship Resources, 1992), p. 1.

15. Koenig, *New Testament Hospitality*, p. 8.

16. Following the lead of Dieter Georgi, *Theocracy in Paul's Practice and Theology* (Minneapolis: Fortress Press, 1991), cf. pp. 36, 45, 85, we have used the term "solidarity" in this book to designate the concepts associated with the Greek term *dikaiosune*, which is more commonly translated into English using the terms "righteousness" (usually among Protestant interpreters) or "justice" (more commonly among Catholic interpreters). None of the terms available to us in English captures the richness or

tality and solidarity are integrally related concepts and practices. God's solidarity with humankind is the foundation for our sharing of hospitality with one another, even as hospitality is a means to the realization of solidarity. God demonstrates solidarity with humankind most clearly in the incarnation, in which Jesus divests himself of his divine privilege, becoming not only human but a slave, and dying obediently the death reserved in the Roman Empire for the lowest forms of humanity (Philippians 2:6-11). The Gospel accounts describe Jesus' solidarity not only with his disciples, but especially with the "unclean," the children, the disreputable women, the sick and the poor — with the outcasts of his society. These relationships brought Jesus into conflict with the religious and political authorities of his day, culminating in his death and resurrection.

In the incarnation, crucifixion, and resurrection of Jesus Christ,

---

conveys without distortion the sense carried by *dikaiosune* and its cognates. In the wider culture, unfortunately, it is no longer clear what "righteousness" conveys, except perhaps a religious state of being, or the disposition of being a "goody-two-shoes." It resonates more positively among church people, but still without much clarity. In common parlance "justice" has come to mean something like "fairness" or "equality" or "what the law says is right," all of which may be fine attributes, but miss the deeply relational aspect that the term carries in the New Testament when used to describe God's (and Jesus') character, and what God hopes of us. Although the term "solidarity" carries its own distracting linguistic baggage, we know of no other word in English that better describes how God seeks to relate to humankind, as well as what God asks of us in our relationships with one another.

We also recognize that many people in North American culture associate the term solidarity with the political realm, particularly with Marxist or socialist politics, as, for example, in the Solidarity Union movement in Poland a few years ago, and may even have an aversion to this term precisely because of these associations. We have used the term "solidarity," nonetheless, precisely to suggest something of the political dimension connoted in Greek by *dikaiosune*, which "righteousness" and "justice" do not convey as clearly or accurately. By "political" we mean the aspect of human experience that has to do with the structuring of relationships (as in the connotations more commonly associated with the "polity"), without presupposing by this any particular political (ideological) orientation (e.g., Democrat vs. Republican).

For a rich and nuanced discussion of the issues pertaining to the translation of *dikaiosune*, see J. Louis Martyn, *Galatians*, The Anchor Bible, 33A (New York: Doubleday, 1997), pp. 249-50, 263-75. There is, of course, a virtually inexhaustible abundance of exegetical and theological studies of righteousness/justice/rectification/solidarity. Martyn's bibliography supplies an abundance of resources for those wishing to wade further into this discussion.

God's solidarity with us thus reconstructs the broken world — making possible our continuing solidarity with God and with one another, and providing a model for us follow. From this model several important insights arise. First, solidarity requires not just "presence" (torturers, after all, are present with their victims), but "struggling on the side of" and "self-giving love."[17] Second, as an expression of God's oneness, the solidarity that God grants to us and seeks of us requires that we abandon expressions of identity that privilege one human constituency — whether Greek or Jew, male or female, slave or free (Galatians 3:28), or conservative or liberal, godly or ungodly — over another.[18] This does not imply the denial of the unique and particular elements of our createdness;[19] God's solidarity reaches out for us whoever we are, without regard for our worthiness or human status (Romans 2:11; 3:21-31).[20]

Third, solidarity comes to life in an array of practices — such as forgiveness, thanksgiving, prayer, and reconciliation — that together with hospitality constitute the primary elements of Christian worship. Solidarity, then, is not merely a state of being, but a way of life. It is both who we are and what we do in the presence of God and because of God's solidarity with us.

God's solidarity with us is not only the foundation and model for our life together, but the basis of our hope for the world that is coming into being. As the ground and focus of Christian hope, divine solidarity and self-giving love also serve as the basis for our participation with God in the reconstruction of human space. It is important to nuance this carefully, however. We do not accomplish the reconstruction of human space and relationships by our own efforts. God's solidarity with us in the cross has *already* shaken the foundations of the world, making a "new creation" (2 Corinthians 5:17-21), reconciling us in one body (Ephesians 2:16), and thereby fundamentally reshaping the whole created order. Our role is to discern and participate with God in this reality.

17. See Volf, *Exclusion and Embrace*, pp. 24ff.

18. See Paul W. Meyer, "The Worm at the Core of the Apple: Exegetical Reflections on Romans 7," in *The Conversation Continues: Studies in Paul and John in Honor of J. Louis Martyn*, ed. Robert T. Fortna and Beverly R. Gaventa (Nashville: Abingdon, 1990), pp. 69ff., and Martyn, *Galatians*, pp. 570-72.

19. We are grateful to our colleague, Dr. Marcia Riggs, for her patient, persistent, and gracious reminders of the importance of particularity.

20. Martyn, *Galatians*, p. 271.

Finally, as we discern God's solidarity with us, our own lives become contested spaces. When the social constructions of fallen humanity dominate our vision, we will "see" alienation, segregation, violence, and despair. This perspective on reality inevitably compels us to seek our own security, to secure "salvation" on our own terms, to close doors and put up walls. Because of our limited human vision, we become captive to the broken and destructive social constructions of the fallen creation. When God, in full solidarity, breaks into this reality, the whole "cosmic landscape" is fundamentally altered, enabling us to recognize our need for deliverance from the malignant powers that hold us captive.[21] From this perspective, our own practices of solidarity and hospitality are not the means by which *we* bring a different social construction into being, but rather the reconstruction and relocation of our vision and practices to the spaces where God's solidarity becomes real and apparent.

In other words, solidarity and hospitality are not practices we pursue in order to fix the problem of poverty or even to accomplish reconciliation between rich and poor people. They are, rather, practices we pursue because they are the "natural" thing to do within the transformed landscape of God's reign. They presume the accomplishment of God's new creation of human space, even as they bring it to concrete expression. Hospitality and solidarity are celebrations of our deliverance from bondage to the broken powers of this world, even as they bring that reality into being. From this vantage point, it becomes clear that solidarity and hospitality are as much about our own transformation as about the transformation of the stranger; they are the "sites" where these transformations can take place. Genuine Christian solidarity and hospitality thus transcend condescending charity, bringing wholly new relationships — one new humanity in Christ — into being.

God's Reconstruction of Reality and the Church

The social reconstruction of reality that is accomplished in Jesus Christ and comes to expression in the pages of the New Testament includes several features that further challenge our prevailing notions and

21. Martyn, *Galatians*, pp. 272f.

practices of "church." First, the earliest Christians apparently understood themselves not so much as a self-contained religious institution, distinguishable from the social structures around them, but as participants in the movement of God's redeeming presence *into* and *within* the structures of the world.[22] Walter Wink has described aspects of this in his argument that "the powers will be redeemed." As he contends, the Christian faith is not about escape from this world, but the redemption of the whole world, including all of the broken and corrupting social institutions of the principalities and powers.[23] The early Christians thus took on at times the appearance of a "voluntary association," at times a "trade guild," and, still more often, a "household." The church was, in fact, all of these and more. We have in the pages of the New Testament such a diverse array of images for the church in part because Christians moved into and contested so many different social spaces in their world.[24]

Second, this contesting of social space also entailed constant social movement and transformation, rather than static institutional self-definition. Several other factors follow. In keeping with this prevailing sense of movement, the earliest Christian communities appear, for the most part, to have been less concerned with boundary maintenance than is typical for the modern church.[25] They may also have understood that God's people, the church, consists primarily of social practices and, thus, exists wherever people gather across social boundaries to celebrate and give witness to God's solidarity with us. In other words, practices such as forgiveness and hospitality appear to have

22. The common dichotomy between institutions and movements can be misleading. Movements do not exist without institutionalized features. The question is whether the institutional features so come to define a movement that the possibility of movement into new social spaces is limited.

23. Walter Wink, *Engaging the Powers: Discernment and Resistance in a World of Domination* (Minneapolis: Fortress, 1992), pp. 73-85.

24. See Paul S. Minear, *Images of the Church in the New Testament* (Philadelphia: Westminster, 1960); John Driver, *Images of the Church in Mission* (Scottdale, Pennsylvania: Herald Press, 1997).

25. The tendency of ancient Mediterranean people to articulate identity in relationship to a central focus, a householder or Jesus Christ, for example, rather than by the articulation of boundaries vis-à-vis other groups and institutions, also plays a significant role in the permeability and mutability of the early Christian congregations.

been more definitive of the church than any particular essentialist form or structure of organization and governance.

Finally, human social constructions based on geographical, political, cultic, ethnic, and racial factors, for example, apparently did not define the earliest church. Because of their conviction that God was renewing all of creation, the early Christians resisted even the distinction between sacred and profane. Perhaps this resistance to factors that constituted walls and closed doors between people in the larger culture enabled them not only more readily to embrace the stranger, but to embrace as well the identity of aliens, exiles, strangers, and slaves as their own (see, for example, 1 Peter 2:11; Philippians 1:1).

In all of these ways, we can begin to see the impact of solidarity and hospitality among the early Christians upon the social construction of space — that is, upon the experience of God's presence and the ordering of human relationships. The picture becomes clearer still if we look briefly at one of the primary social sites in which this all came to expression among the early Christians, namely at table.

Contesting Space at the Table

Eating is a universal human activity. In this culture we tend to regard eating primarily as a biological function, leading us sometimes to overlook its inescapable social dimensions. Whether we eat alone or with others, at home or in a restaurant, vegetarian or beef, as we eat we presume, express, and embody a wide range of values, customs, social and economic arrangements, and assumptions about the world and our place in it. Mealtime is, in fact, a form of social theater, both describing and inscribing social reality and the ordering of relationships. A meal taken at one of our popular fast food restaurants, for example, presumes a complex set of global economic arrangements, the management of workers spread across thousands of miles, and political decision-making by people we have never met. Thousands of people have their fingers somewhere in our food — winners and losers in the arrangements that end at our table. The manner of our eating says a lot about us. Do we dine in, eat in the car, or take our food home? How do we interact with those who stand on the other side of the counter, or with other guests around us? Do we resist or prefer the company of strangers? Will we dine only with those of our own race or class? These and countless other questions we usually resolve without a second thought, unaware of the social theater in which we act.

In the world of Jesus and Paul, meals were particularly rich with social drama. In the households of the Roman Empire, the evening meal was an occasion to demonstrate the honor of the patron. The number and status of the invited guests, the quality and abundance of food served, and the seating arrangements in the dining area were all elements in the script. Slaves, women, children, and perhaps even some of the people invited to dinner typically ate outside the proper dining area (the *triclinium*), and may have consumed lesser-quality food, thereby demonstrating their lower station in life relative to those eating in proximity to the host. Just as the architecture of the Roman house itself focused attention on matters of status,[26] so also mealtime arrangements addressed the same concerns, demonstrating, for all to see, not only the status of the patron and household as a whole, but the hierarchy of relationships within.

Just under the surface of these arrangements, a worldview that presumed differing levels of humanness — distinctions between male and female, slave and free, patron and client, father and child — was always at work. The social construction of mealtime thus mediated to all present a powerful story of the way the world works. In this story, the ordering of nature dictated that some were powerful and free, others weak and servile. As the philosopher Aristotle had put it, ". . . the household in its perfect form consists of slaves and freemen."[27] At the meal, in the grand script and in countless details, this story was told over and over and over again.

Against this background we can begin to see more clearly the reasoning behind Paul's stress on the importance of the stories being

---

26. See especially, Andrew Wallace-Hadrill, "The Social Structure of the Roman House," *Papers of the British School at Rome* 56 (1988): 43-97. Among many discussions of the ancient meal, see Osiek and Balch, *Families in the New Testament World*, pp. 193-214; Peter Lampe, "The Eucharist: Identifying with Christ on the Cross," *Interpretation* 48, no. 1 (January 1994): 36-49; Dennis E. Smith and Hal E. Taussig, *Many Tables: The Eucharist in the New Testament and Liturgy Today* (Philadelphia: Trinity Press International and London: SCM Press, 1990).

27. Aristotle, *Politics* I 1253b.

told and enacted at meals in Christian households. In 1 Corinthians 11:17-34, he apparently challenges Christians who in word and deed are mingling different stories, thereby mangling the Christ story. When the Corinthian Christians gather to celebrate the Lord's Supper, they apparently continue to follow at least some of the conventions of status differentiation typical of pagan meals, so that some are drunk and others hungry, or, in other words, some have more than they need, while other do not have enough (11:21). Even as they proclaim aloud their oneness in Christ's body, their practice betrays a story — a social construction of reality — that is full of factions, status, snobbery, and humiliation (11:18-19, 22). As Paul notes, this must not be the table of the Lord after all (11:20).

In response to what he perceives as a crisis of identity and practice, Paul recalls the tradition he had received and passed on to them. At the table of the Lord, which was also beset by betrayal, a story is told of thanksgiving to God (who supplies all that we need for life), of broken bodies and a new covenant sealed by the Messiah's blood (11:23-25). Thanksgiving, brokenness, new covenant, and the blood of the cross stand in contrast to arrogance, status, and division. Paul reminds the Corinthians that their meal together is a remembering, a fresh enactment and proclamation of the Lord's death, that anticipates the fulfillment of the promises of new creation when he comes again (11:25-26). This is the story they must not only tell, but perform together.

Paul's argument here presumes that mealtime is, in fact, not only social theater, but the performance of a different understanding of reality. It is space that must be contested, for wherever brokenness prevails, God's reign has not yet been realized. His own perspective is enlivened by the reality of the Spirit of the crucified and resurrected Christ in his life, transforming his identity and all of his relationships. He understands that arrogance and factions are the sacraments of the "flesh," the powers of fallen creation. The Lord's table, where unity, thanksgiving, and the solidarity of the cross prevail, constitutes holy space in the presence of the God of Jesus Christ. For Paul, the Lord's table is the very essence of hospitality and solidarity, a reclaiming of broken space from hostile powers.

The same convictions drive the confrontation with Cephas that Paul recounts in Galatians 2:11-14. Here Paul contends that Cephas's withdrawal from table fellowship with Gentiles, following a visit from James's followers, constitutes a betrayal of "the truth of the gospel" (2:14). Why? Perhaps because the decision not to share table with the Gentiles reinscribes exclusive expressions of identity, essentially relegating Gentile Christians to second-class status in the family of God. Here again the drama being enacted is one of division rather than solidarity. New creation has been brought up short. The solidarity we discern and practice at the Lord's table, in contrast, requires that we leave ethnic identity and religious scruples at the door.

Paul's admonition to Cephas is consistent with what we can discern regarding Jesus' practice of table fellowship. Among many of Jesus' contemporaries in Israel, such as the Pharisees, for example, access to the table was typically determined around questions of purity. The Gospels portray Jesus repeatedly challenging by his actions any distinctions based on exclusive notions of purity, which divide God's people into insiders and outsiders. For Jesus, God's purity is manifested in restoration, healing, and unity, for God is one. Jesus' public practice of table fellowship with tax-collectors and sinners (e.g., Matthew 9:9-13, pars.) provokes outrage among the Pharisees not only because it disturbs custom, but because it implicitly challenges the prevailing assumption that God's holiness and purity come to expression in exclusion. As Matthew's account suggests, Jesus' peculiar practice of table fellowship is consistent not with the social construction of division, but with God's merciful solidarity. Holiness is oneness, not division. This mission of divine solidarity, therefore, necessarily focuses on the inclusion of sinners, those who are excluded in the current social and religious arrangements. Hospitality through table fellowship is simply the most natural expression of Jesus' understanding of God's person, albeit one that defies the logic, worldview, theological convictions, and practices of the religious insiders.

Throughout the Gospels, Jesus' practices and teachings about table fellowship reflect powerful convictions about God's mercy and solidarity with humankind. By his practices and teaching he persistently contests the social constructions of the religious leaders, which are imposed upon and dominate the imagination of the people. If this organization of reality is to be disrupted and Israel made whole again, the whole system of domination and exclusion must be unmasked. When he shares a meal with his disciples on the night of his betrayal, Jesus brings his tradition of table fellowship in solidarity with the broken to its culmination, and also grants to his disciples the vision of an alternative reality rooted in the story of a God who dies on the cross. At the Last Supper (Matthew 26:26-29, pars.) Jesus juxtaposes the suffering and death that await him — the perfect expression of God's solidarity with the suffering of the world — with new covenant, forgiveness, and the anticipation of God's reign — God's reconstitution of the world in solidarity! — about to come into being.

In the world that Jesus anticipates at the Last Supper and that comes into being at the cross, humankind is able to live together in perfect communion with one another and with the Creator. Because God is revealed to us at the cross in complete solidarity with our humanity, suffering, and mortality, the distance between God and humankind has been completely erased. At the cross, God's solidarity with us is perfected. As a consequence, every practice, every thought, and every human construction driven by our alienation from God is rendered obsolete.

When Christians gather at table today they continue the tradition that began with Jesus and the first Christians. It is a tradition of resistance to and subversion of the powers of this world. It unmasks the hollow logic and vain constructions of fallen humanity, contesting and disrupting all the spaces where alienation and domination still prevail. The table tradition makes the hope of God's reign a reality amidst the voices of despair, and brings healing and reconciliation to those who know only violence and hate. It opens every closed door.

Remarkably, all of this happens in the most common event — a simple meal. Amidst the principalities and powers, a meal may seem small and ineffective. But, as we have discovered on the streets, such small, embodied signs of God's reign show us the way and give us hope for the journey. At the basement door of Butler Street Church, in the yard at 910, at the dumpsters by the morgue, in the labor pools, on the benches in Woodruff Park, and in the halls of Grady Hospital — in all of these places where we have shared time, space, or a meal with strangers, we have seen glimpses of Christ bringing the beloved community into being. As Ed Loring often says, "Justice is important, but supper is essential."[28]

28. Written for this volume by Stan Saunders.

Study for "Junkyard Mandala"
Monotype; 30" × 15"; © 1996 Christina Bray

About the Artist

The art in this book is taken from Christina Bray's exhibit, *Street Prayers/Spiritual Journeys*, which appeared at Columbia Theological Seminary in the fall of 1999. Bray's richly symbolic prints are composed of images and scenes from inner-city Atlanta, where she grew up. Exploring her own spiritual journey and theological convictions in the urban context, Bray has created a series of urban images focusing on prayer and social justice. More specifically, Bray is interested in how art itself may act as intercessory prayer for marginalized persons. "One of the strongest themes in my images," she says, "is the marginalization of poor people in urban areas, particularly homeless people."

Bray has a Bachelor of Fine Arts degree from Atlanta College of Art and a Masters of Fine Arts from the University of Georgia, where she concentrated on printmaking and book arts. She also has a Master of Theological Studies degree from Candler School of Theology at Emory University. Christina Bray currently resides in Lawrenceville, Georgia.

Artist's Statement

My creative work encompasses two major objectives: the personal and the theological. The former, of course, is more private, while the latter is more public. More specifically, I seek to do two things through my art. The first is to convey a sense of my own history, spirituality, hopes, fears, etc. Much of this ongoing self-portrait is based on my roots in inner-city Atlanta and an empathy toward the hardships faced therein. The second is to apply visual art to the work of the Christian assembly, namely to Christian worship. Liturgical theology is of significant interest to me as an artist because it delves into all areas where art can serve the church: public worship, social justice, Christian education, and aesthetics. I create paintings, drawings, and prints that humbly attempt to contain these personal and theological elements; many of the images contain the overarching theme of prayer.

The evolution of my current work began in 1995, when I took two significant courses as a graduate student at the University of Georgia. The first was an art history course on spirituality in modern art. It led me to consider the spiritual deficit in my own life and to begin incorporating spiritual elements into my work. The second was a drawing course where students' work was based on studies of their childhood memories and environments. My work focused solely on the East Atlanta neighborhood of my childhood, which was no stranger to crime and poverty. I sought to convey an insider's view of the environment by taking an empathetic stance rather than a critical one. By 1996, I had

178

begun reading some theology and was working on a series of urban images on prayer and social justice.

As my interest in Christian theology grew, I began a conversion experience. I needed to incorporate more theological themes into my work but did not have the proper religious education. In the fall of 1997, I enrolled in the Master of Theological Studies program at the Candler School of Theology and have since explored how art-making is a form of ministry. Art can function as prayer both for the Christian community and for the artist, and it enriches the worship experience of Christians at both the communal and personal levels. More specifically, visual art is a potent language for praise, supplication, and intercession—all of which are key types of prayer in the Christian liturgy. In much of the art I made in seminary, intercession for the poor and marginalized was a major theme. More recently, I am coming to understand that this work is also autobiographical and self-critical; it is an honest way of exploring who I am (or should be) in terms of Christian faith.

Some examples of my work include *Epiphany,* where a stray cat symbolizes a spiritually or materially impoverished person receiving God's grace; "Somebody Lives Here," where a condemned house provides shelter for those who must *live* in the *unlivable;* "Blessed Are the Poor in Spirit," which emphasizes God's solidarity with the poor; and "A Dream about a Shelter," which is based on an actual dream I had about a chapel in the wilderness. My most recent work is the "Prayer Wall series, a collection of paintings of graffiti-covered inner-city walls where elements of private devotion and collective worship emerge.

Christina Bray
December 1999

Select Bibliography

Abbott, Edwin Abbott. *Flatland: A Romance of Many Dimensions.* 6th ed. Princeton: Princeton University Press, 1991; New York: Dover Publications, 1953.

Abramsky, Sasha. "When They Get Out." *The Atlantic Monthly* 283, no. 6 (June 1999): 30-36.

Aulén, Gustaf. *Christus Victor.* New York: Macmillan, 1931.

Avila, Rafael. *Worship and Politics.* Translated by Alan Neely. Maryknoll, NY: Orbis Books, 1981.

Bakirtzis, Charalambos, and Helmut Koester, eds. *Philippi at the Time of Paul and after His Death.* Harrisburg, PA: Trinity Press International, 1998.

Bales, Kevin. *Disposable People: New Slavery in the Global Economy.* Berkeley: The University of California Press, 1999.

Blau, Joel. *The Visible Poor: Homelessness in the United States.* New York: Oxford University Press, 1992; Oxford paperback, 1993.

Bonhoeffer, Dietrich. *The Cost of Discipleship.* Translated by R. H. Fuller. Rev. ed. New York: Macmillan, 1959.

Brown, Colin. "Ernst Lohmeyer's *Kyrios Jesus.*" In *Where Christology Began: Essays on Philippians 2,* edited by Ralph P. Martin and Brian J. Dodd, 6-42. Louisville, KY: Westminster/John Knox Press, 1998.

Brueggemann, Walter. *Finally Comes the Poet: Daring Speech for Proclamation.* Minneapolis: Fortress Press, 1989.

———. *The Prophetic Imagination.* Philadelphia: Fortress Press, 1978.

Campbell, Debra. "A Catholic Salvation Army: David Goldstein, Pioneer Lay Evangelist." *Church History* 52 (1983): 322-32.

———. "'I Can't Imagine Our Lady on an Outdoor Platform': Women in the Catholic Street Propaganda Movement." *U.S. Catholic Historian* 3 (1983): 103-14.

Davidson, Joe. "Caged Cargo." *Emerge* 9, no. 1 (October 1997): 36-46.

Day, Dorothy. *The Long Loneliness*. 1952. Reprint San Francisco: HarperSanFrancisco, 1981.

Driver, John. *Images of the Church in Mission*. Scottsdale, PA: Herald Press, 1997.

Elliott, Michael. *Why the Homeless Don't Have Homes and What to Do About It*. Cleveland: Pilgrim Press, 1993.

Fowl, Stephen E., and L. Gregory Jones. *Reading in Communion: Scripture and Ethics in Christian Life*. Grand Rapids: Wm. B. Eerdmans Publishing Co., 1991.

Frei, Hans W. *The Identity of Jesus Christ: The Hermeneutical Bases of Dogmatic Theology*. Philadelphia: Fortress Press, 1975.

Gans, Herbert J. *The War Against the Poor: The Underclass and Antipoverty Policy*. New York: Basic Books, 1995.

Gathje, Peter R. *Christ Comes in the Stranger's Guise: A History of the Open Door Community*. Atlanta: Open Door Community, 1991.

Georgi, Dieter. *Theocracy in Paul's Practice and Theology*. Minneapolis: Fortress Press, 1991.

Gilens, Martin. *Why Americans Hate Welfare*. Chicago: University of Chicago Press, 1999.

Gregory, Derek. *Geographical Imaginations*. Oxford and Cambridge, MA: Blackwell, 1994.

Gundry-Volf, Judith M., and Misoslav Volf. *A Spacious Heart: Essays on Identity and Belonging*. Harrisburg, PA: Trinity Press International, 1997.

Gutíerrez, Gustavo. *The Power of the Poor in History*. Maryknoll, NY: Orbis Books, 1983.

Hall, Edward T. *The Hidden Dimension*. New York: Doubleday, 1966.

Harvey, David. *The Condition of Postmodernity*. Oxford and Cambridge, MA: Blackwell, 1990.

———. *Justice, Nature and the Geography of Difference*. Oxford and Cambridge, MA: Blackwell, 1996.

Hauerwas, Stanley. "The Politics of Freedom: Why Freedom of Religion Is a Subtle Temptation." In *After Christendom? How the Church Is to Behave If Freedom, Justice, and a Christian Nation Are Bad Ideas*. Nashville: Abingdon Press, 1991.

Horsley, Richard A., ed. *Paul and Empire: Religion and Power in Roman Imperial Society*. Harrisburg, PA: Trinity Press International, 1997.

Kaku, Michio. *Hyperspace: A Scientific Odyssey through Parallel Universes, Time Warps, and the 10th Dimension*. New York and Oxford: Oxford University Press, 1994.

Kellermann, Bill Wylie. "Bill, the Bible, and the Seminary Underground." In *Radical Christian and Exemplary Lawyer*, edited by Andrew W. McThenia, Jr., 56. Grand Rapids: Wm. B. Eerdmans Publishing Co., 1995.

———. "Listen to This Man: A Parable before the Powers." *Theology Today* 53 (October 1996): 299-310.

———. *Seasons of Faith and Conscience: Kairos, Confession, Liturgy*. Maryknoll, NY: Orbis Books, 1991.

King, Martin Luther, Jr. "Letter from Birmingham City Jail." In *A Testament of Hope: The Essential Writings of Martin Luther King, Jr.*, edited by James Melvin Washington, 300. San Francisco: Harper and Row, 1986.

King, Mernie. "Like Street Preaching in Downtown Rome: Witnessing at Nuclear Weapons Facilities." In *Waging Peace: A Handbook for the Struggle to Abolish Nuclear Weapons*, edited by Jim Wallis, 206-12. San Francisco: Harper and Row, 1982.

Koenig, John. *New Testament Hospitality: Partnership with Strangers as Promise and Mission*. Philadelphia: Fortress Press, 1985.

Koontz, Gayle Gerber. "The Liberation of Atonement." *Mennonite Quarterly Review* 63 (April 1989): 171-92.

Lampe, Peter. "The Eucharist: Identifying with Christ on the Cross." *Interpretation* 48, no. 1 (January 1994): 36-49.

Lash, Nicholas. "Performing the Scriptures." In *Theology on the Way to Emmaus*. London: SCM Press, 1986.

Lefebvre, Henri. *The Production of Space*. Oxford and Cambridge, MA: Blackwell, 1991.

Levenson, Holly. "Atlanta's Hardest Working People: A Report on Day Labor Pools in Metro Atlanta." Atlanta: Atlanta Labor Pool Workers' Union, 1998.

Lischer, Richard. *The Preacher King: Martin Luther King, Jr. and the Word That Moved America.* New York: Oxford University Press, 1995.

Lohfink, Gerhard. *Jesus and Community: The Social Dimension of Christian Faith.* Philadelphia: Fortress Press, 1984.

Malina, Bruce J. *The New Testament World: Insights from Cultural Anthropology.* Rev. ed. Louisville: Westminster John Knox, 1993.

Malina, Bruce J., and Jerome H. Neyrey. *Portraits of Paul: An Archaeology of Ancient Personality.* Louisville: Westminster John Knox Press, 1996.

Martyn, J. Louis. *Galatians.* The Anchor Bible, 33A. New York: Doubleday, 1997.

McClure, John S. *The Roundtable Pulpit: Where Leadership and Preaching Meet.* Nashville: Abingdon Press, 1995.

McThenia, Andrew W., Jr., ed. *Radical Christian and Exemplary Lawyer.* Grand Rapids: Wm. B. Eerdmans Publishing Co., 1995.

Meeks, M. Douglas. *God the Economist: The Doctrine of God and Political Economy.* Minneapolis: Fortress Press, 1989.

Meeks, Wayne A. "The Man from Heaven in Paul's Letter to the Philippians." In *The Future of Early Christianity: Essays in Honor of Helmut Koester,* edited by Birger Pearson, 329-36. Minneapolis: Fortress Press, 1991.

Meyer, Paul W. "The Worm at the Core of the Apple: Exegetical Reflections on Romans 7." In *The Conversation Continues: Studies in Paul and John in Honor of J. Louis Martyn,* edited by Robert T. Fortna and Beverly R. Gaventa, 62-84. Nashville: Abingdon, 1990.

Minear, Paul S. *Images of the Church in the New Testament.* Philadelphia: Westminster, 1960.

Mishel, Lawrence, Jared Bernstein, and John Schmitt. *The State of Working America, 1998-1999.* Ithaca: ILR Press/Cornell University Press, 1999.

Moltmann, Jürgen. *The Way of Jesus Christ: Christology in Messianic Dimensions.* Translated by Margaret Kohl. San Francisco: HarperSanFrancisco, 1990.

Moorman, John R. H. *Saint Francis of Assisi.* London: SCM Press, 1950.

Myers, Ched. *Binding the Strong Man: A Political Reading of Mark's Story of Jesus.* Maryknoll, NY: Orbis Books, 1988.

Newman, Katherine S. *No Shame in My Game: The Working Poor in the*

Inner City. New York: Alfred A. Knopf and the Russell Sage Foundation, 1999.

Olgetree, Thomas. *Hospitality to the Stranger: Dimensions of Moral Understanding*. Philadelphia: Fortress, 1985.

Orfield, Gary, and Carole Ashkinaze. *The Closing Door: Conservative Policy and Black Opportunity*. Chicago: University of Chicago Press, 1991.

Osiek, Carolyn, and David Balch, *Families in the New Testament World: Households and House Churches*. Louisville: Westminster John Knox, 1997.

Palmer, Parker. *The Company of Strangers: Christians and the Renewal of America's Public Life*. New York: Crossroad, 1981.

Pomerantz, Gary M. *Where Peachtree Meets Sweet Auburn: A Saga of Race and Family*. New York: Penguin Books, 1996.

Richard, Pablo. *Apocalypse: A People's Commentary on the Book of Revelation*. Maryknoll, NY: Orbis Books, 1995.

Rose, Lucy Atkinson. *Sharing the Word: Preaching in the Roundtable Church*. Louisville: Westminster/John Knox Press, 1997.

Rutheiser, Charles. *Imagineering Atlanta: The Politics of Place in the City of Dreams*. New York: Verso, 1996.

Sawicki, Marianne. *Seeing the Lord: Resurrection and Early Christian Practices*. Minneapolis: Fortress Press, 1994.

Schlosser, Eric. "The Prison-Industrial Complex." *The Atlantic Monthly* 282, no. 6 (December 1998): 51-77.

Slawson, Douglas J. "Thirty Years of Street Preaching: Vincentian Motor Missions, 1934-1965." *Church History* 62 (1993): 60-81.

Smith, Christine M. *Preaching as Weeping, Confession, and Resistance: Radical Responses to Radical Evil*. Louisville: Westminster John Knox Press, 1992.

Smith, Dennis E., and Hal E. Taussig. *Many Tables: The Eucharist in the New Testament and Liturgy Today*. Philadelphia: Trinity Press International and London: SCM Press, 1990.

Smith, Louis, and Joseph Barndt. *Beyond Brokenness*. New York: Friendship Press, 1980.

Soja, Edward W. *Thirdspace: Journeys to Los Angeles and Other Real-and-Imagined Places*. Oxford and Cambridge, MA: Blackwell, 1996.

Stone, Clarence N. *Regime Politics: Governing Atlanta, 1946-1988*. Lawrence, KS: The University Press of Kansas, 1989.

Stringfellow, William. *An Ethic for Christians and Other Aliens in a Strange Land.* 3rd paperback ed. Waco, TX: Word Books, 1979.

————. *Free in Obedience.* New York: Seabury Press, 1964.

————. *A Keeper of the Word: Selected Writings of William Stringfellow.* Edited by Bill Wylie Kellermann. Grand Rapids: Wm. B. Eerdmans Publishing Co., 1994.

————. *My People Is the Enemy: An Autobiographical Polemic.* New York: Holt, Rhinehart, and Winston, 1964.

————. *A Private and Public Faith.* Grand Rapids: Wm. B. Eerdmans Publishing Co., 1962.

Thistlethwaite, Susan B., and George F. Cairns, ed. *Beyond Theological Tourism: Mentoring as a Grassroots Approach to Theological Education.* Maryknoll, NY: Orbis Books, 1994.

Volf, Miroslav. *Exclusion and Embrace: A Theological Exploration of Identity, Otherness, and Reconciliation.* Nashville: Abingdon Press, 1996.

Wallace-Hadrill, Andrew. "The Social Structure of the Roman House." *Papers of the British School at Rome* 56 (1988): 43-97.

Weaver, J. Denny. "Atonement for the Nonconstantinian Church." *Modern Theology* 6 (July 1990): 307-23.

Willimon, William H. "Christian Ethics: When the Personal Is Public Is Cosmic." *Theology Today* 52 (October 1995): 366-73.

Wilson, William Julius. *When Work Disappears: The World of the New Urban Poor.* New York: Alfred A. Knopf, 1996.

Wink, Walter. *Engaging the Powers: Discernment and Resistance in a World of Domination.* Minneapolis: Fortress, 1992.

————. *Naming the Powers: The Language of Power in the New Testament.* Philadelphia: Fortress Press, 1984.

————. "Neither Passivity nor Violence: Jesus' Third Way." *Forum* 7 (March/June 1991): 5-28.

————. *Unmasking the Powers: The Invisible Forces That Determine Human Existence.* Philadelphia: Fortress Press, 1986.

Wray, Harmon. "Dungeons for Dollars? The Trend Toward Prisons for Profit." *Hospitality* 18, no. 1 (January 1999): 1-2.

Wuthnow, Robert. "What Religious People Think About the Poor." *The Christian Century* 111 (September 7-14, 1994): 812-16.

Yoder, John Howard. *Body Politics: Five Practices of the Christian Commu-*

nity Before the Watching World. Nashville: Discipleship Resources, 1992.

———. *The Politics of Jesus.* Grand Rapids: Wm. B. Eerdmans Publishing Co., 1972.

Index of Names and Subjects

Index of Scripture References